THE FORMULA

THE PROVEN & UNBREAKABLE SYSTEM TO QUICKLY GROW YOUR BUSINESS

STEVE HACKNEY

Foreword by

Sir Clive Woodward

THE FORMULA

THE PROVEN & UNBREAKABLE SYSTEM TO QUICKLY GROW YOUR BUSINESS

© 2019 STEVE HACKNEY

All rights reserved. No part of this book may be reproduced in any form or by any means without the written permission of the publisher (except by a reviewer, who may quote brief passages and/or show brief video clips in a review).

ISBN 978-0-9567907-2-9

Published in the UK by TCA Publishing

To support local families and children, TCA Publishing donates a percentage of all book sales to the Rainbows Hospice for Children and Young People.

DEDICATION

To my wife, Helen, for giving me unwavering support through all the highs and lows and for giving us our three wonderful children, Thomas, Matthew and Liv.

To my mum and dad, who inspired me to go after my dreams, to work hard and to never, ever give up.

And to Peter, my long-term business partner and friend, without whose incredible support, generosity and amazing business acumen, none of this would have been possible. Thanks, mate.

TABLE OF CONTENTS

CHAPTER 1: An Introduction To The Formula 27

T – Transform the Results of Existing and New Strategies 28

L – Lead-Generation Strategies 35

C – Conversion Strategies 36

M – Maximise Customer Value 37

S – Systemise 39

CHAPTER 2: The Magic Behind The Formula 43

CHAPTER 3: Transform Existing Sales And Marketing Tactics, And Strategies 49

1. TARGET MARKET 52

2. DIFFERENTIATOR 76

3. HEADLINE 92

4. IRRESISTIBLE OFFER 101

5. FEATURES AND BENEFITS 115

6. GUARANTEE 118

7. REASONS WHY 124

8. SOCIAL PROOF 127

9. CALL TO ACTION 130
CHAPTER 4: The World's Most Successful Sales And Marketing Strategies For Any Business 137
CHAPTER 5: Lead Generation 143
The Importance of Your Irresistible Offer 149
LEAD-GENERATION STRATEGY 1: Joint Ventures 155
LEAD-GENERATION STRATEGY 2: Website 169
LEAD-GENERATION STRATEGY 3: Google Ads 187
CHAPTER 6: Conversion 213
Creating a Sales Conversion System 222
CHAPTER 7: Maximising Customer Value 237
Creating Your Maximising Customer Value System 242
The Customer Penetration System 255
The Referral System 260
Up-Sell and Cross-Sell 266
Monthly Printed Newsletter 275
CHAPTER 8: Systemise 281
The 'Growth Continuum' 283
Automating Your Lead Generation 284
Automating Your Conversion 285
Automating Your Maximising Customer Value 292
Automating Your Entire Business 293
CHAPTER 9: Your Biggest Problem … Solved 295
CHAPTER 10: Conclusion … Accelerate 303
ACCELERATE YOUR BUSINESS 304

ACKNOWLEDGEMENTS

There are so many people I want to thank for sharing their ideas, tactics and strategies with me. My learning has never stopped since I read my first sales and marketing book by the brilliant Drayton Bird, *How to Write Sales Letters That Sell.*

I also want to thank the hundreds of coaching and consulting clients who have worked with me through the years, especially the first few, who took the leap of faith!

Plus, the tens of thousands of business owners around the world who have helped to shape this book, and the tactics and strategies contained in its pages. Without you, none of this would be possible. Thank you too for putting your faith in me and my team.

I'd also like to thank my 'Business Growth Experts'. You inspire me every day to keep improving all our systems and strategies to ensure the business owners we work with throughout the world get the results they deserve... and get them quicker than they could ever have previously wished for.

I'd also like to thank a number of amazing people who have been business partners or mentors (in no particular order)...

To Richard (Brewin) for teaching me how to run successful businesses and never giving up on me. To Grant (Eagle) for helping me to master online marketing and so many other things! To Simon (Organ) for teaching me so much about sales and now video production. To Ric (Wilson) for sharing your wonderful insights into business processing. To Howard (Flint) – your systems and procedures, and their detail, inspired me to put systems above pretty much everything. To Simon (Cohen) for being my agent when playing rugby and for being there for me ever since. To Clive (Woodward) – thank you so much for writing the Foreword. You were an inspiration to me in your playing days at the Tigers, even more so when you took England from also-rans to world champions and ever since with your determination to get people to push the boundaries of performance in business and in sport. Thanks, Clive.

And last but by no means least, I want to thank my business partner and friend Peter Finlay. Your support has been unwavering. We've built several businesses together over the years ... some great, some average and some which didn't even make a penny (that's what being an entrepreneur is all about!).

We've kissed a few frogs, but together as entrepreneurs we've helped a lot of people realise their dreams and ours, too. None of this would have been possible without you Pete.

FOREWORD

By Sir Clive Woodward

Winning ... it's been at the heart of everything I've done since my early days at school.

Whether in sport or in business, my entire philosophy has been based on one simple formula: work hard, lay the right foundation, and model and implement what the best are doing.

Do that, and you'll outperform the competition.

This approach has served the people and teams I've been lucky enough to work with along the way, extremely well.

Not least, the England rugby team!

So why am I writing the Foreword for a business book by Steve Hackney?

There are two reasons:

Firstly, I've known Steve since he first played for me back in my England days and have come to know what a successful professional he was then and is now.

But the second is the most compelling reason, and that's this book is also about improving performance and winning.

And this time it's about YOUR PERFORMANCE, and it's about YOU WINNING the marketing game for your team and for your business.

For example, so many business books don't go far enough. They stop short at telling you exactly what you need to do to win in the subject area that they cover.

They omit key details and leave you hanging.

This book is different.

You see, whether you like it or not, your success in the 'field of battle' comes down to not just what you do, but HOW YOU DO IT.

That's the 'game of success'.

This book takes one of the most measurable, powerful and up-to-date formulas available to grow a business (your business in this case) and shows you HOW TO APPLY IT to your advantage and to win, and win big.

In my experience, when you combine multiple high-performance tactics, as Steve has done here, that's when you start to see positive changes in whatever you're doing.

For example, in my pursuit of winning, I brought in the best specialists for every facet of the game: from defence coaches to kicking coaches, dieticians to doctors. When we won the World Cup, I had a team of 'experts' that numbered 18.

It's fair to say Steve has done the same thing here for you in the context of growing your business.

I would go as far to say he has given you what I would call a 'success blueprint' in the following pages.

Enjoy this book, and use it to create a game plan that will see you achieve your own goals.

One thing is for sure: you will be richer for the experience.

WHAT THIS BOOK IS ABOUT (AND WHAT IT'S NOT ABOUT)

Hello, my name is Steve Hackney.

Before we start I thought it would be a good idea to introduce myself and quickly explain what this book is about and more importantly what it's NOT about.

This book is NOT about using the next bright shiny button (the next new sales or marketing tactic, like a new social media platform), although this book will ensure you get maximum results from it.

This book is NOT about giving you theories. I've read enough business books (more than 2,000 of them!) to know when the author is trying to 'pull the wool over your eyes'. Everything you read in these pages is therefore proven in the 'field of battle'. Absolutely nothing is an idea for you to 'try out'.

This book is NOT about you having to spend a considerable amount to multiply your sales and profits. Much of what I take you through can be done without cost, or on a shoestring.

Of course, it's impossible to grow entirely without cost, but I can assure you, no matter how good or bad your cash flow is right now, it won't affect your results... as long as you implement what follows.

If you are currently unhappy with your growth, or struggling to generate clients, customers or patients you may think you've got a growth problem. But in my experience, after working with thousands of businesses, I've found that almost every growth problem is just a symptom of a much greater problem, a problem that's very easy to fix.

That's the good news!

Not long ago I was in a coaching meeting with one of my personal clients... Shafiq.

He runs a small accounting firm.

They have been going a few years and have around 50 business clients. Like many business owners, Shafiq thought he had a lead-generation problem, but like the legions of businesses we work with, I knew it wasn't a lead-generation problem; it was a SYSTEM problem.

In other words, he doesn't have an easy-to-apply business growth 'FORMULA' in place which builds his business on autopilot.

After listening to Shafiq tell me about his challenges, I sat back and said, 'look, the good news is you don't have a lead-generation problem. You just need to put in place a business growth system based on a proven formula that leverages the five key components of your business. Right now, you're trying to tap into just one of them – lead generation – and doing it unsuccessfully. But when you apply THE FORMULA everything changes in an instant.'

Over the last six months Shafiq has applied THE FORMULA and the business has more than doubled in size, with very little increase in costs.

In my experience (and it's the same with dozens and dozens of our coaches) most business owners simply don't understand what makes marketing work and what areas of the business to focus on to bring about growth, more sales and more profit.

That's your opportunity… no matter how large or small your business is.

In all likelihood, you too have little understanding of what makes marketing work and what elements of your business you should focus on to bring about **quick and big increases in sales and profits**… and achieve it with very little, if any, extra cost.

That's not a criticism; it's the reality of running a business. You're good at delivering whatever product or service you sell, and business growth is just something that doesn't come naturally to many people. In fact, it's something I had to work extremely hard at for a long, long time, before I was able, with complete certainty, to tell any business owner what they needed to do to grow.

It takes years and years to learn this stuff (and I'm still learning!), just like your area of expertise.

So what did Shafiq do to double the size of his accountancy firm in six months, without increasing his costs? Well, that's what this book is about.

This book takes you through 'THE FORMULA' and dissects each of its five elements to give you a blueprint to building your business as quickly as you want.

The book then shows you how to apply THE FORMULA in your business and what you have to do to automate it.

Once you understand the fundamentals of THE FORMULA, I'll then take you through the strategies and tactics to maximise each of its five key elements.

What you'll discover (and it's a pleasant surprise) is that growing a business, though not rocket science, is nevertheless a science (primary school level).

Finally, you'll also get what I call a *success formula* for each tactic and strategy, so you can easily apply it to your business. I've found that dissecting even complex things into bite-sized parts makes it so easy to apply; and, more importantly, that you'll get results faster.

When you implement and apply THE FORMULA to your business, you'll see it transform before your very eyes, ensuring you take advantage of the five growth elements, allowing you to multiply your sales and profits, and to dominate your competition.

That's what this book is about.

INTRODUCTION

I'll admit it, I was lucky when I started my first business. It was November 1995. At the time I was a professional rugby player for Leicester Tigers (one of Europe's most successful rugby union clubs).

Rugby had turned professional only that summer, just after the Rugby World Cup in South Africa. I was 27. I knew I probably only had three or four years left as a pro, so I decided to set up my first business, Hackney Marketing.

I say 'lucky' because often when people set up their first business, they take huge risks.

You may have been the same.

I didn't take any.

I was getting paid a decent professional rugby player's salary. At that point I was an established player. I'd been on several England tours, played for England in the Hong Kong Sevens and turned out a number of times for the famed Barbarians, so I was earning around £90,000 (modest compared to today's professional contracts). Therefore, unlike so many people starting out in business, I didn't need the business to generate income immediately.

Only a few months earlier I had been the sales and marketing manager for a large commercial insurance brokers. Prior to that I had sold photocopiers for Canon. I'd been relatively successful at both, and so the natural consequence when rugby went professional was to set up my own marketing company.

But, as you know, running a business is entirely different to being a 'technician' in another business (Michael Gerber's *E-Myth Revisited* on this phenomenon is a must read), so it was a steep learning curve.

I also quickly realised I didn't really know that much about sales and marketing. Sure I'd had success, but going out and advising people how to build their businesses was another matter.

So I got my hands dirty. We were training just a couple of times a day, so I had a huge amount of spare time on my hands. Back then, Jeff Bezos had just started Amazon.com (July 1994), and I quickly became one of his best customers. Back then, Amazon was 'Earth's Biggest Book Store', and I invested in literally hundreds of sales and marketing books from them. I was like a kid in a candy store!

I learned how to speed read and created files on my computer arranged into two main folders: one for sales and one for marketing. I then added more folders for each sub-topic and created my own library of 'dynamite sales and marketing tools, tactics and strategies'. Anything I read that I thought sounded good, I added it to the relevant folder and file. I was building up a bank of what I thought were killer strategies that I could unleash on my first crop of consulting clients. I went to seminars (webinars weren't around back then, so I travelled sometimes long distances, even to the USA, to learn what worked).

I acquired my first set of consulting clients about 18 months after starting my 'information overload', and I was armed and ready.

But to my surprise, much of what I applied for my clients didn't work. And things that worked for one client, didn't work for another.

I started taking the things that worked and 're-modelled' them, tested them again, and, when they worked, looked to improve them.

You see, the problem back in the late 90s was that there wasn't an 'end-to-end' system for growing businesses – there was a gap in the market.

After another year or so of testing and improving my own modified strategies, I created my first-ever marketing system. It was called 'The POWER Marketing System'.

And because no other system existed back then for any small or medium sized business which could take the business owner step-by-step through what they needed to do to grow their businesses, it was a massive hit. We would print and pack five large manuals in a box and ship them all over the world. I sold thousands and thousands of them in 46 different countries.

I retired from rugby in 1999, by which time I had already built a very successful international sales and marketing business.

And things went from strength to strength.

Then, through a mutual client, I met Peter, my business partner. It was December 2004. He had asked me to speak at one of his business growth events in early 2005. Pete, at that time, was (and still is) one of the world's most successful franchise, licensing and business modelling experts. After the event he asked me if I could spare an hour or so to discuss a business idea he had.

His idea was to build a franchise consultancy business based on the franchise models he had created over the years (for the likes of BT and many others), and he asked if I'd like to join him (and Howard, Pete's other business partner back then) and help them grow it.

I must admit, I loved everything about it, and I knew with my business growth system in hand we would build it quickly. In fact, from a standing start in January 2005, we built it to become Europe's largest franchise consultancy group and sold it in September 2007 to a business consortium for several million pounds.

That was real, first-hand experience of the power of using a business-building system and the effect it can have on a business when you get everything set up correctly.

More importantly, it was during these years and working with more than 65 franchisors in every imaginable sector that I started to lay the foundation that would become what I now call 'THE FORMULA'. However, I was a long way from creating something that would work for every imaginable business.

After a short sabbatical, Pete and I then decided to put THE FORMULA to use and take it to businesses everywhere. My accountant and good friend Richard Brewin (one of my original consulting clients) had coincidentally just sold his accounting firm (for a high-end multiple), and in a meeting where he was introducing Pete and me to the new owners of the firm, asked what we were going to do now. We told him that we had decided to get THE FORMULA to the small and medium sized business sector, and he said simply, "You should do that via accountants, and I'll help you".

So that's what we did. Over the next eight years we built the world's largest sales and marketing network for accountants. More importantly, we gave each of our members the rights to provide access to all their business clients to my marketing system.

With more than 1,500 accountants worldwide, each with, on average, 250 business clients, we exposed my business growth system to tens of thousands of business owners, and our accountants were reporting back on their results.

It was arguably one of the largest test of its kind ever conducted.

But that was just the start.

What emerged was a real insight into the tactics and strategies that were working for everyone. Equally, there were several tactics and strategies that were hit-and-miss. And unfortunately there were also tactics and strategies that just didn't work, no matter what we did.

Crucially, out of all the tests, I identified a pattern, a formula, if you like. The most successful businesses used certain elements, and combined together they were giving them the highest returns, the fastest growth and the most profit. The difference it made was staggering. And that's when I dug deeper and found THE FORMULA that was actually already there in my system but hidden. It's this FORMULA that the rest of the book is all about.

It's the culmination of over 20 years of growing businesses, the result of probably thousands upon thousands of mistakes (I've learned more through my mistakes than the stuff that worked!). It's the culmination of tens of thousands of businesses applying my tools, tactics, strategies and FORMULA.

I wanted to write this book because I don't believe any business owner has ever been given a proven, end-to-end step-by-step FORMULA that is guaranteed to grow their business, no matter what they sell or where they are in the life cycle of their business.

I'm passionate about helping the owners of small and medium sized businesses because, let's face it, growing a small or medium sized business isn't easy. But there is an easier way, and that's when you use THE FORMULA.

Far too many businesses go bust, not in the main because the products or services aren't good, but because the owners don't have the skills, knowledge or expertise to market the business successfully.

My hope is that after reading this book, you'll be one step closer to reaching your goals and ambitions, and you'll create a thriving business that helps you multiply your sales and profits and ensures you dominate your competition.

WHY THIS BOOK IS DIFFERENT

By investing in this book, you've put your faith and trust in me as your coach. I know you're busy; I know you're immersed in your business; I know how valuable your time is to you. But I'm delighted and honoured that you have decided to spend your time with me on this journey, and I won't waste any of your time – I promise. This book is different from any other business book you may have read, in three important ways…

1. **Everything I Share with You Is Timeless:** I reveal only strategies, tactics and concepts that have stood the test of time and will never grow old or stop working. THE FORMULA itself is evergreen. It will never stop working, and it will never need to change.

   Remember the good old fax machine and the Yellow Pages? These media are all but extinct. I used to absolutely love the Yellow Pages. I've made literally hundreds of thousands from ads in the Yellow Pages directories. I even created a best-selling step-by-step manual called *The Wipeout Technique*, which sold for £127. People lapped it up. It showed how to create amazingly powerful ads in the Yellow Pages. But that's pretty much obsolete now.

   You're getting timeless strategies, concepts and tactics that will work forever!

2. **I Practice What I Preach:** I don't have one FORMULA for you and one for me. I don't have tactics or strategies that aren't good enough for me, but good enough for you (or vice versa).

Everything – and I mean everything – in this book is as relevant to me, my clients, my coaches and their clients as it is to you. If you were given an insight into my businesses, you'd see that I follow THE FORMULA and everything in it... to the letter. Seriously, this works. That's why I use it day in, day out. That's why my private clients use it. That's why tens of thousands of other business owners use it.

I do this for real.

If you've ever attended one of my seminars you'll see me deliver content in line with what I'm about to reveal to you. I live and die by THE FORMULA and 'practice what I preach'.

3. **Simple, Quick and Easy Implementation:** In addition to giving you THE FORMULA, you'll notice every tactic or strategy comes with its own success formula. I've found through experience and through all the tests we've run (and continue to run) that there are certain essentials that need to be used to ensure a tactic or strategy works at an optimal level.

   So, to make it as easy for you as possible, I give you the exact formula to use and then explain, step-by-step, each component part of THE FORMULA.

   Where possible, I also give you a proven example and a template you can apply to your own business. You won't have seen anything as comprehensive as this before, no matter how many books you've read or how many seminars you've attended.

I recommend you read the book from start to finish first. Take notes. Underline the things that jump out at you. Then dive into the chapters you believe will give you the biggest results first. Then, and most importantly, start implementing THE FORMULA in your own business.

Okay. Let's get started...

CHAPTER 1:

AN INTRODUCTION TO THE FORMULA

$$(T \times L \times C \times M)S$$

= EXPONENTIAL BUSINESS GROWTH

THE FORMULA is very simple and easy to apply. In this chapter I'm going to explain why it works so well and take you through its component parts, so that by the end of this chapter you'll have a thorough understanding of it. The following chapters will then focus on each of the parts that make up THE FORMULA.

First, let me take you through each of the main parts...

T – Transform the Results of Existing and New Strategies

(**T** × L × C × M)S = EXPONENTIAL BUSINESS GROWTH

To start with you need to TRANSFORM the results and performance of EVERY sales and marketing strategy you're CURRENTLY using and those you add in the future.

To do this you must deploy something I call the *Core Elements*.

This is the science of marketing. The *Marketing DNA*.

The Core Elements are based on the results over the last two decades from thousands and thousands of tests, and they are the foundation of all SUCCESSFUL sales and marketing.

The best way to think about the Core Elements is that they are the things that make marketing work.

In my experience, I would say that 99.9% of people don't really know what makes marketing work. I believe this is the first time you will ever have had it explained in a way that will enable you to understand it easily and then be able to evaluate and then transform all your marketing as a result.

There are nine Core Elements: five *Marketing Elements* and four *Sales Elements*.

The Marketing Elements are...

1. Target Market
2. Differentiator
3. Irresistible Offer

4. Guarantee
5. Social Proof

The Sales Elements are

1. Headline
2. Features and Benefits
3. Reasons Why
4. Call to Action

The diagram on the next page shows how the Sales and Marketing Elements work together to produce highly successful sales and marketing strategies.

***

At this stage, don't concern yourself with the detail of what each Core Element is and how to apply it – I'll take you through each of the elements in Chapter 3. What's important right now is that you have a basic understanding of the Marketing DNA and the nine Core Elements that make marketing work.

Armed with the nine Core Elements, you can apply them to all of your existing tactics and strategies, and to new ones as you create them. I guarantee this will result in a massive transformation in the success of each strategy, which in turn obviously generates extra sales and profits for you and your business.

And here's the thing...

THE FORMULA

The Marketing DNA – The Nine Core Elements

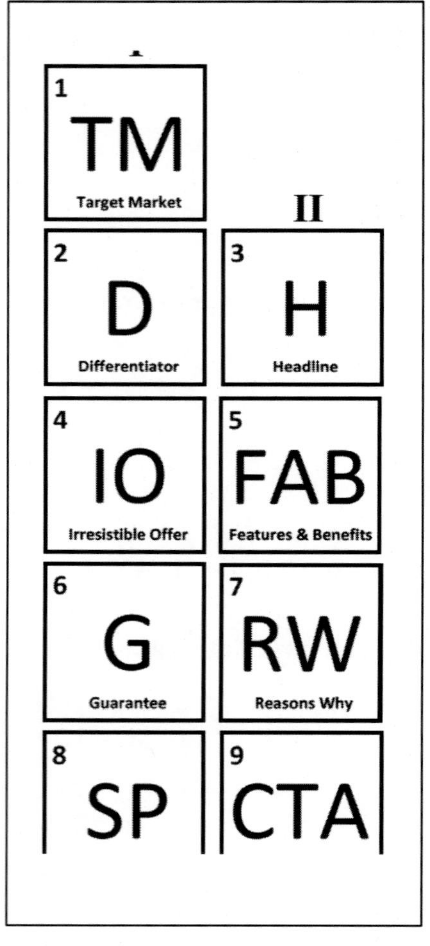

Copyright © The Core Asset Limited

The nine Core Elements DO NOT cost a single penny to incorporate into your tactics and strategies.

Think about that for a second.

No matter what sales and marketing strategies you're using right now, you can transform their effectiveness WITHOUT spending a penny more.

Here's a good example.

The next page shows a conventional agency-designed ad for a company that produces revolutionary devices for the printing industry.

This is a typical ad.

This ad flopped. It flopped because there are just a couple of Core Elements used, both of which are deployed poorly.

In other words, its Marketing DNA is flawed. As a result, it breaks down and doesn't work.

It's the same with websites, letters, postcards, leaflets, inserts, emails – you name it. If it's a sales and marketing tactic or strategy, then the likelihood is it will be highly deficient when it comes to using the Core Elements. Therefore, it's Marketing DNA is flawed, and results are poor.

This is NOT rocket science, but it IS a science.

A typical ad created with little or no use of the Core Elements.

All you have to do to get enhanced and often spectacular results is to ensure you include the Core Elements. It's that simple.

The ad shown on the next page and several like it, helped to create a multi-million pound business virtually from scratch – that's the difference it can make when you apply the Core Elements to all your marketing.

If all you did right now was transform your existing strategies by applying the Core Elements to them and ensure new ones you launched also included them, then this alone would have an instant and significant impact on your business.

This is why I'm telling you everything in this book is timeless. The Core Elements will never stop working. They will always be the Marketing DNA. Of course, new media and new tactics will spring up as time goes by (think... Facebook, Twitter, LinkedIn, WhatsApp etc.) but as long as you apply the Core Elements to those media and tactics you'll always get great and often transformational results.

THE FORMULA

Now you can save thousands of pounds each year and improve the quality of your work...

"They Laughed When I Put The Tri-Creaser On My Folding Machine, But When They Saw The Results..."

"It's so frustrating. Even the so called leading manufacturers haven't come up with a creasing device that eliminates cracking on many materials.

And we have to out source most of our folding and creasing. It costs us thousands each year as well as hours and hours each week."

Have you heard yourself saying the same things? Despite all the technological advances we're making - no-one has solved the age old problem of fibre cracking. Okay some machines work 40-50 percent of the time - but is this good enough?

The Solution: A Simple And Very Effective Device

I agree it's unacceptable. So about two years ago I decided to do something about it. After 78 prototypes (yes, I don't give up easily) I finally achieved my goal. I created the "Tri-Creaser," - a rotary creasing device that **totally eliminates fibre cracking** on materials ranging from 150 gsm to 350 gsm.

Already **hundreds** of printers and print finishers are benefiting from using the Tri-Creaser. Here's what a few of them have said...

"Your Tri-Creaser is simple - easy to use, and works on a wide variety of stocks. It has saved me some £100 - £200 perweek."
Mr J Cole, **Eden River Press Ltd**

"The Tri-Creaser is simple to use with 100% quality. On average it saves us £30,000 per annum."
Mr B Tucker, **BRG Print Finishers**

"The Tri-Creaser is very straight forward - operator picked it up quickly. 80% of our scoring is now done in house."
Mr D Vokins, **Hunts Printing**

As you can see the Tri-Creaser is achieving **startling** results. And we have

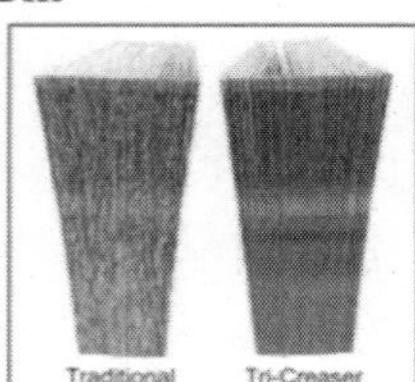

Tech-ni-Fold's "Tri-Creaser" is guaranteed to totally eliminate fibre cracking

"Secret" Creasing Agent Is The Key

So why hasn't anyone made this "discovery" before?

That's simple really. The Tri-Creaser uses a **"secret"** specially formulated creasing agent that stretches the fibres (doesn't crush like all other methods). Therefore fibre cracking just isn't "allowed" to occur.

You're now probably thinking, "Great, no more cracking, but I bet it takes ages to set up!" Here's the really good news...

Takes Just A Few Minutes To Set Up

The Tri-Creaser takes just **minutes** to set up even by inexperienced operators. In fact the Tri-Creaser takes the skill out of quality creasing operations, so no one needs any training.

The operator is given **simple instructions** on how to adjust the settings to the stock thickness. All this takes is just a few minutes! Better still...

Attaches To All Popular Folding Machines

The Tri-Creaser attaches to all popular

Here are some more important benefits...

- **The Tri-Creaser doesn't need demonstration.** It will start saving you time and money the moment you open it.
- **All the settings (3 creasing widths, and 2 deep settings) are built-in to the design** so theTri-Creaser is like having a very specialised operator working tirelessly for you, hour after hour, day after day, week after week - without the cost
- **The Tri-Creaser will crease as fast as your folding machine can run.** It is 100% effective even over 25,000 sheets per hour!
- **You'll never have to outsource straight creasing jobs again.** Massive savings in time and money!
- **Superb for normal section work**
- **Excellent on digital stock**
- **Pays for itself on average between 1 and 3 job runs**

The Tri-Creaser also comes with a unique money back guarantee.

I'm not asking you to order today. Send for our **FREE "Tri-Creaser Information Kit."** I'll give you all the details. Only then do you have to make up your mind.

Call us now on [redacted] or complete the coupon below and post it to us at the address below. Do it now. You really will be surprised at the vastly improved quality of your creasing work as well as the savings you'll make!

☐ Yes! Please send me your FREE Tri-Creaser Information Kit.

Name: ____________________

Company: ____________________

Address: ____________________

____

Tel: ____________________

The new ad, created with all the Core Elements

IMPORTANT NOTE:

There's nothing 'creative' about this ad. It just includes the Core Elements (the DNA), and, as a result, has generated millions in sales across the world.

Of the five parts of THE FORMULA, this is without doubt THE most important. That's because the Marketing DNA also needs to be applied to the 'L', 'C' and 'M' parts of THE FORMULA to maximise their results too.

Now let's move on to the second component of THE FORMULA...

L – Lead-Generation Strategies

(T × **L** × C × M)S = EXPONENTIAL BUSINESS GROWTH

The lifeblood of every business is its ability to generate a constant supply of leads or enquiries. Without leads, you can't acquire clients, customers or patients.

Lead generation, however, is often (not always) the most expensive way to grow a business. So you need to add as many cost-effective and proven lead-generation tactics and strategies as you can – the more the better. In Chapter 5 I'll take you through some of my favourites.

The more successful strategies you use, the quicker your business will grow.

This could be as simple as sending out a series of great emails, executing a Google Ads campaign or sending a direct mail campaign.

Of course, as I mentioned in the Introduction, there are best-practice ways to implement all these strategies.

As I said, I call them *success formulas*, but of course each success formula is underpinned by the Core Elements (the Marketing DNA). You'll see the success formulas scattered throughout this book.

It's not difficult to create lead-generation strategies like this when you follow the success formulas.

Your goal is to launch as many cost-effective ones as you can, ones that give you a return on investment.

Let's now take a look at the third component of THE FORMULA...

C – Conversion Strategies

(T × L × **C** × M)S = EXPONENTIAL BUSINESS GROWTH

Just being able to generate a constant flow of leads isn't enough. Once you've acquired them, you now need to convert as many of those leads as possible into paying clients, customers or patients.

You do that using a number of conversion tactics and strategies.

These are tactics and strategies which help move the lead through to becoming a customer, ideally at the right price or fee.

For very little or no extra cost, you can get more clients, customers or patients from the leads you generate, maximising your return on investment on all your lead-generation tactics and strategies.

The chances are, you currently focus very little time or attention on conversion. Once you do, and you follow my advice in Chapter 6, you'll be pleasantly surprised at how easy it is to transform your conversions. It really is very easy to do.

M – Maximise Customer Value

(T × L × C × **M**)S = EXPONENTIAL BUSINESS GROWTH

Once you've acquired the client, customer or patient, you then need to maximise their value.

Without doubt, this is the most neglected part of almost every small and medium sized business. I don't mean businesses neglect their clients, customers or patients; I mean they neglect the money-making potential of them.

There are four key areas that will help you maximise customer value:

1. Increase frequency of purchase (getting clients, customers or patients to buy more often).
2. Increase referrals (getting clients, customers or patients to recommend you more often).
3. Increase average order value (increasing the value of every sale).
4. Reduce attrition (keeping hold of clients, customers or patients for longer).

Your customer list is one of the most valuable assets your business will ever have. In other words, there's G-O-L-D in your customer list – you just need to learn how to extract it!

I know for certain that if you're NOT capitalising on your most valuable asset (your clients, customers or patients), then you're in for a REAL treat!

For example:

As I mentioned in the Introduction, over the last eight years or so we have worked with more than 1,500 accounting firms all over the English-speaking world: Small firms with 1–3 partners.

Our main membership programme cost £500 a month, with our best members paying a one-off 'Lifetime Membership' fee of £14,997. Other members paid £9,995 to become 'Accounting Mentors', whilst hundreds of other members paid thousands more on other products and services we created for them.

Therefore, the value of each member is not just the 'basic' £500 a month, it's all the other products and services they bought along the way, together with all the other people they referred to us.

Believe me, it's easy to get existing customers to buy these other products and services. The hardest part (and even that's not too challenging) is coming up with the extra products and services in the first place!

Remember, the real cost is the initial expense to acquire your clients, customers or patients. After that, the costs are virtually nil to extract further sales and revenue from them, and that's why this component of THE FORMULA will bring you your biggest leverage and returns!

Obviously, if you've just started your business, you currently won't have many clients, customers or patients. But you must still focus on this part of THE FORMULA. Why? Because as you add more and more clients, customers or patients, you need to ensure you maximise their value. Now is the perfect time to focus on this part of your business.

Okay. Now let's look at the fifth component, the 'S'...

S – Systemise

$(T \times L \times C \times M)^{S}$ = EXPONENTIAL BUSINESS GROWTH

So far we've covered the first four elements of THE FORMULA. They will become the backbone of your entire business.

They will provide your business with...

Solidity

Growth

Profit

...and ensure it's immune to outside forces, such as your competition and a changing economy.

However, to take it to an even higher level, one that accelerates your growth even faster, you need to systemise and then automate these four elements.

In other words, you get them working even while you're asleep or on holiday!

Notice the 'S' sits outside the brackets. If you know anything about mathematics and formulas, that means the 'S' multiplies the effect of EVERYTHING inside the brackets. It really is that powerful and effective.

Often, one of the real drawbacks of running a small or medium sized business (and you know this all too well) is that there just aren't enough people in the business to do everything that's required, so you end up working long hours, which impacts on every other area of your life.

By systemising and then automating the growth of your business, you reduce the reliance on people, free up a huge chunk of time for yourself and ensure your business keeps moving forward at pace.

Furthermore, systemisation and automation reduce human mistakes and enhance results.

So it's a win-win-win.

Okay. So how do you systemise and automate without needing to be a professor of sorts or needing expensive software? Well, there are several simple ways, and we'll discuss them all in Chapter 8.

Finally, you'll have noticed that the first four components of THE FORMULA are each separated by a multiplication sign:

$$(T \times L \times C \times M)S$$

It's the **'MULTIPLICATION EFFECT'** that provides the real magic behind THE FORMULA. So much so, the next chapter is dedicated to it.

Chapter Summary

- THE FORMULA:

$$(T \times L \times C \times M)S$$

$$=$$

EXPONENTIAL BUSINESS GROWTH

(T – Transform Existing and New Strategies × L – Lead Generation Strategies × C – Conversion Strategies × M – Maximize Customer Value) S – Systemise

- There are **Nine Core Elements**:

Five *Marketing Elements* and four *Sales Elements.*

The **Marketing Elements** are...

1. Target Market
2. Differentiator
3. Irresistible Offer
4. Guarantee
5. Social Proof

The **Sales Elements** are

6. Headline
7. Features and Benefits
8. Reasons Why
9. Call to Action

THE FORMULA

- There are four key areas that will help you Maximise Customer Value:

    1. **Increase frequency of purchase** (getting clients, customers or patients to buy more often).
    2. **Increase referrals** (getting clients, customers or patients to recommend you more often).
    3. **Increase average order value** (increasing the value of every sale).
    4. **Reduce attrition** (keeping hold of clients, customers or patients for longer).

CHAPTER 2:

THE MAGIC BEHIND THE FORMULA

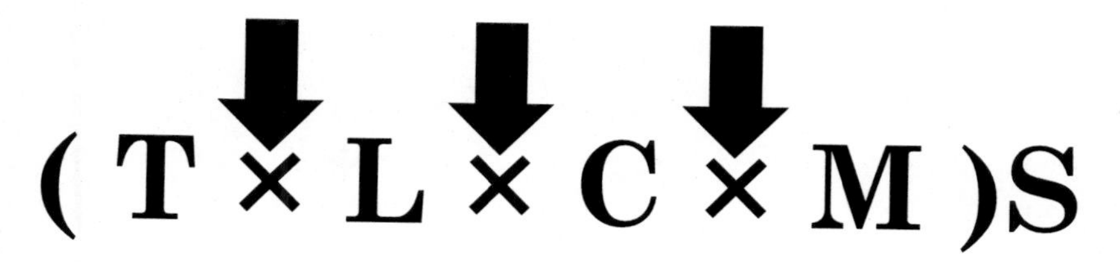

= EXPONENTIAL BUSINESS GROWTH

he multiplication effect of THE FORMULA provides the real 'magic'. What that means is that all the components are interrelated, so as you add more tactics and strategies within each component and optimise each one, the result is multiplied. That's lost on many people.

It's the hidden gem of THE FORMULA and the reason it's so successful.

The result is you get exponential growth rather than linear growth.

Here's a simple example to show you the power of THE FORMULA (it's important you understand this, because it explains why your results will be achieved far quicker than you may ever have imagined).

Let's say, right now, you are generating 100 leads a month. You convert 25 of those into customers. Each sale is worth, on average, £500. You don't do anything else to maximise sales from customers. That means you're generating £12,500 a month.

Are you with me so far?

Okay. Now let's say you've completed this book and you start taking massive action (more on this later, the great Tony Robbins calls this a 'MAP' – Massive Action Plan).

First, you transform your existing strategies.

You transform the performance of your lead-generation tactics and strategies.

You transform the conversion of your leads so you get more clients, customers or patients.

And you transform your customer maximisation tactics and strategies.

And let's keep things simple and say you transform all those components by just 20% (believe me that's a drop in the ocean compared to what's possible).

So now your numbers look like this:

COMPONENT	CURRENT (month)	AFTER 20% IMPROVEMENT
Lead Generation	100	120
Conversion	25%	30%
Customer Maximisation	£500	£600
TOTAL TURNOVER	£12,500	£21,600

WOW!

By 'tweaking' (and 20% is definitely just 'tweaking') your lead-generation, conversion and customer maximisation components by just 20%, you've increased turnover by 72.8%.

And you've done it with zero extra spend.

So that's Stage 1 complete. Remember, all you've done so far is focus on the 'T' of THE FORMULA: Transforming Existing Tactics and Strategies.

You now move on to adding more lead-generation tactics and strategies (L), more conversion tactics and strategies (C), and more customer maximisation tactics and strategies (M). In the following chapters I'll take you through my favourites, so it will be easy for you to add more tactics and strategies across these three components of THE FORMULA.

Once again, for the purpose of illustration, let's keep the numbers simple.

By adding more tactics and strategies, you improve each component by a mere 10% (once again this is a drop in the ocean compared to what's possible, but I'm keeping the numbers low so you can see the power of what you've now got). Here's what your numbers look like now:

COMPONENT	CURRENT (month)	AFTER 20% IMPROVEMENT	AFTER ADDING MORE TACTICS 10% IMPROVEMENT
Lead Generation	100	120	132
Conversion	25%	30%	33%
Customer Maximisation	£500	£600	£660
TOTAL TURNOVER	£12,500	£21,600	£28,749

Double WOW!

From starting out with a turnover of £12,500, you've increased monthly turnover to £28,749, an increase of almost 130%. On an annual basis, you've gone from £150,000 to a staggering £344,988.

Not too shabby.

The numbers don't lie. I've been more than conservative with the increases, but even if this were all you did each year from this day forward, just think what your business would look like in a few years' time. In fact, think what it would look like in six months' time!

That's the POWER of THE FORMULA.

That's why it's UNBREAKABLE.

That's why it will have a huge impact on your business when you apply it. And we've not even added in the effect of Systemise & Automate (S) yet!

Obviously, you should do this initial exercise with your own business so it feels more real. To make it easy for you, we've developed an amazing online tool called the Business Growth Calculator.

Since you've invested in this book, you can access it FREE here:

www.FreeFormulaBook.com/resources

Hopefully, that shows you what's possible!

Do you see how it's the multiplication effect that gives you EXPONENTIAL growth?

That's the true power of THE FORMULA.

You should be starting to get very excited now.

Armed with THE FORMULA, it's now just a case of implementing it into your own business, and that's what the following chapters concentrate on. Let's start with 'T' – Transform Existing & New Tactics and Strategies ...

CHAPTER 3:

TRANSFORM EXISTING SALES AND MARKETING TACTICS, AND STRATEGIES

$$(T \times L \times C \times M)A$$

= EXPONENTIAL BUSINESS GROWTH

et this right, and you'll never, ever worry about growing your business again. Most business owners don't know what makes marketing work. That's not surprising. There's so much BS out there and, with information overload, it's confusing.

Let's first look at what marketing ISN'T.

It's not social media (although that's becoming increasingly important).

It's not about your brand (although that's very important).

It's not a website (although that's crucial).

It's not what you do (although, of course, that plays a part).

So what is marketing?

Marketing is simply your ability to influence people to buy your products or services.

That's it.

How do you do that effectively?

Well, it's taken me decades of testing to really discover what makes marketing work, but, as I mentioned in Chapter 1, there are nine elements, nine Core Elements that are the Marketing DNA.

These nine elements are the foundation of all your sales and marketing, and as long as they are present in all your sales and marketing strategies and tactics (as you'll see, you won't necessarily use all of them all of the time, but I'll explain what you need to use and when shortly), you'll influence many, many more people to buy from you and keep buying from you.

One book I recommend on the subject of influence is Robert Cialdini's *Influence – The Psychology of Persuasion*, it's a great read and goes into real detail on the aspects of influence.

What I'm going to do now is take you through each of the nine Core Elements. I'll explain exactly what each one is, give you its success formula, and present good and bad examples so you can gain a greater understanding of them, making it easier to apply to your own business.

I can tell you that this level of deep understanding can only be gained after years and years of study, testing and application. I'm going to give you all this on a plate, so you can use it immediately in your business to great effect. I promise that once you've finished this chapter, you'll be armed with the nine most powerful tools on this planet to grow your business, and that you'll be able to use them to achieve anything and everything you ever dreamed.

You'll have noticed that none of the Core Elements are necessarily new to you. For example, I'm pretty sure you've heard of 'features and benefits'. But I can guarantee you won't be using most of the Core Elements, and that those you do use won't be applied correctly or used to maximum effect. And right now, you have no way of knowing what 'good' looks like and how you can transform them so they optimise your results.

Believe me, what follows is pure GOLD, so pay close attention.

And remember, all nine Core Elements are FREE to apply. They don't cost you any more money to apply to your sales and marketing tactics and strategies, yet they have the POWER to *multiply your results*.

That's why, in Chapter 2 when we looked at how THE FORMULA works to exponentially grow your business, I told you the percentage increases in my example were conservative. In my experience, it's not uncommon to get 50%, 100%, 250%, even 500% or 1,000% increases in results when you apply the Core Elements.

So, even if you're using a tactic or strategy that's currently working, when you apply the Core Elements to it or transform the Core Elements already in your specific tactic or strategy, you'll see significant and often exponential gains.

Right, let's dig in...

1. TARGET MARKET

SUCCESS FORMULA:

(I + A + T) = TM

(Identify + Avatar + Tailor) = Target Market

OVERVIEW:

When I'm running seminars or training courses, one question I get asked repeatedly is this: 'Steve, what would you say is the most important thing when it comes to growing a business?'

Without a doubt, it's the target market.

To get the best possible results from each of the other eight Core Elements and the component parts of THE FORMULA, you must first, and most importantly, clearly identify the type(s) of clients, customers or patients you are looking to target. These are typically known as the *target market(s).*

The ideal target market/markets is/are a clearly identified group or groups of people/businesses who/which

1. **Need** – and, more accurately, *want* – your products or services
2. Can **afford to pay** for your products or services
3. Can be **easily reached by your marketing efforts**
4. Have **similarities** (demographic/psychographic) that enable you to 'group' them together.

One of the biggest mistakes you can make is to try to be 'all things to all people'.

Yes, there is success to be found using this approach, but by focusing on one or more carefully chosen target markets, you'll be far more successful, and this success will be achieved much quicker than with any other approach.

Listen: You're running a small or medium sized business. You don't have hundreds of thousands or millions of pounds sloshing around in your business. You need to watch every single penny you spend. You aren't a big brand (not yet anyway).

So why do so many businesses try to be all things to all people? In most cases it's because they're frightened to limit the number of potential customers they specifically target. They think that if they reduce the number of prospects, they'll risk their whole livelihood!

Nothing could be further from the truth. Let me explain.

I'm often asked, 'If I limit my market, won't I be reducing the chances of doing business with more people?'

Yes, you will. But to succeed in today's competitive market place, you need to concentrate your marketing on a small number of well-chosen target markets, into which you pour all of your resources.

Of course, if you focus on a smaller group you may miss the business from outside the target group. But what actually happens is that you increase the amount of business you receive from the target group.

This is because you are specifically meeting the target market's needs and requirements. You are saying to them that you are THE business that knows about their situation, their wants and desires, their problems and challenges, and their concerns. No other business specifically meets their needs in this way, and therefore your business is seen as the logical company to turn to.

So, you must define your target market BEFORE you do anything else.

Traditional Mass Marketing versus Target Marketing

The diagrams on the following two pages show the differences between mass marketing (targeting everyone) and target marketing (targeting a smaller segment of the market)...

The Mass Marketing Approach

Prospects Who Are Unlikely to Buy

The white space represents potential customers that are unlikely to buy, but they all receive the same marketing message from the business, which results in needless and excessive expense.

Universe

The prospects who could buy your products or services – Mass Market.

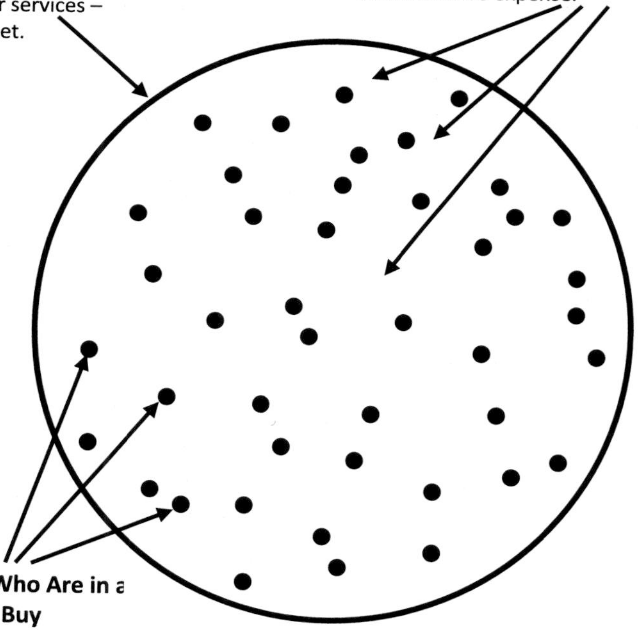

Prospects Who Are in a Position to Buy

Note how disparate these
The white space in betwe
represents everyone else
the mass market. You hav
spend much more money
get 'lucky' and hit the righ
people/businesses.

acquisitions are low, because you're targeting everyone with a 'mass market' message (i.e. it doesn't directly appeal to the buyers). Greater effort (on your part!) required to qualify out bad prospects: if you're targeting everyone, you'll also get a large number of poor

THE FORMULA

The Target Market Approach

: Market Univer

· prospects who cc

Prospects Who Are Unlikely to Buy

The white space represents potential customers who are still unlikely to buy, but they all receive the tailored marketing message from you once tł enquiry has been generated by your marketing efforts. Notice there are fewer now!

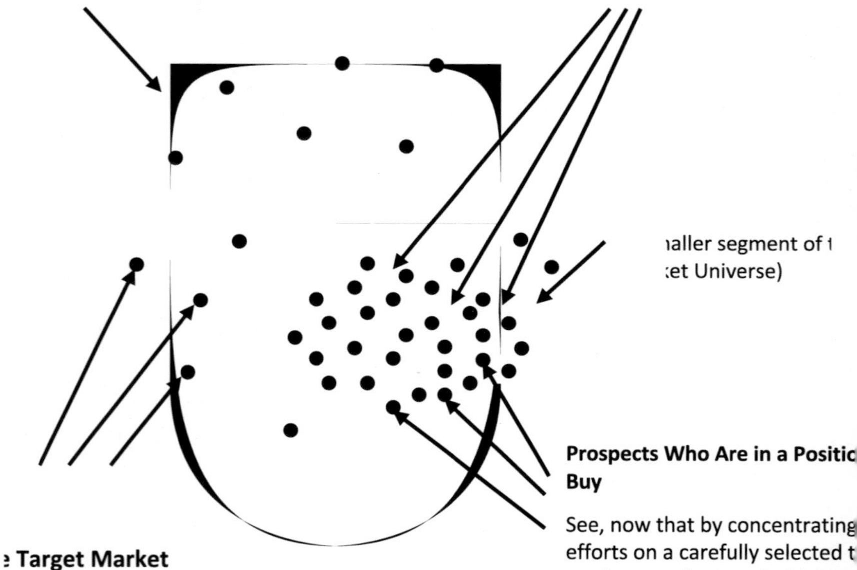

ıaller segment of ı
:et Universe)

Prospects Who Are in a Positic Buy

See, now that by concentrating efforts on a carefully selected t market, you 'capture' a high proportion of potential buyers. once you've generated the enq your message then also needs t completely focused on this gro

: Target Market

:n this approach isn't perfect, but it'
se! You can't hope to 'catch' everyo
:re will still be other people/busines
:side the chosen target market(s) th

he Result

ıis gives you the ability to concentrate your efforts ı
ıore targeted group. Target marketing increases

Multiple Target Markets

You don't have to restrict yourself to just one target market. You may find it necessary to focus on two or more target markets, depending on the products or services you provide. For example, an accountant may have three target markets:

- Start-up businesses
- £500,000–£1 million businesses
- £1 million–£2 million businesses

Or even more defined ('vertical') target markets:

- Dentists
- Media companies
- Legal

The accountant in this example would need to 'speak' and 'communicate' very differently to each target market, because they are so different. An accountant cannot speak the same way to a start-up business as they would to a £2 million business. If you think about it, it's completely illogical, but that's what people do!

Here's a diagram showing how this looks...

THE FORMULA

Multiple Target Markets

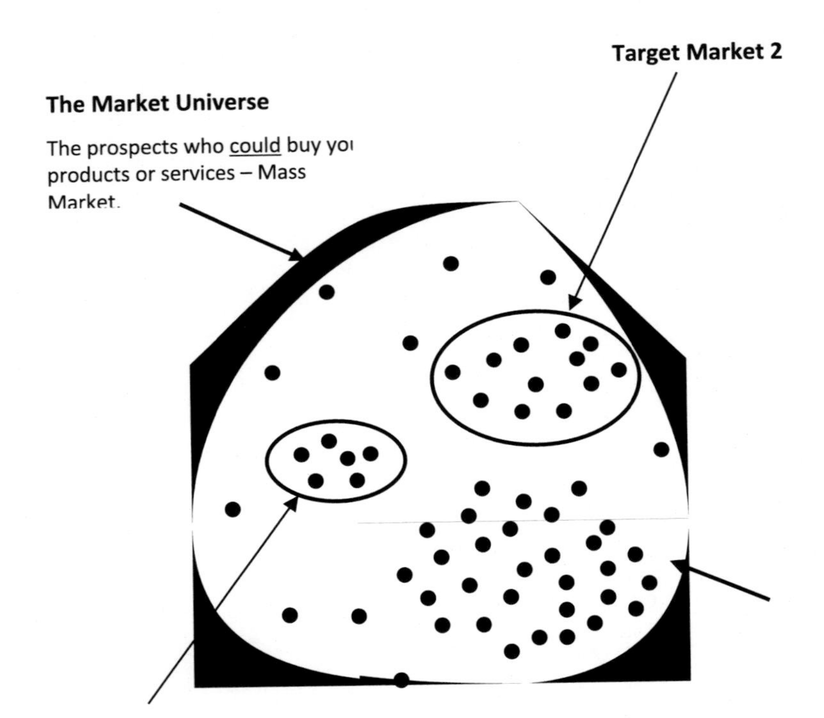

Target Market 2
The Market Universe
The prospects who could buy yo
products or services – Mass
Market.

This gives you the ability to concentrate your efforts on more targeted groups. Target marketing increase the likelihood of a sale and enables YOU to take a big slice of this target market.

The Power of Target Marketing

Here's a simple but very powerful example of why defining your target market is so important.

Let's say a start-up business needs an accountant. Their first choice is to perhaps look in the local newspaper. Although there are a few classified ads, the first one reads:

'ABC Chartered Accountants. Tax preparation, auditing, bookkeeping, payroll services and management accounts for all types of businesses.'

The second ad reads:

'XYZ Chartered Accountants. Specialising in helping start-ups get their businesses running quickly, profitably and effectively.'

Which accountants are they likely to choose?

The answer is obvious. If you can create this bond between your business and the target market(s), I guarantee you'll grow your business quicker than you could ever imagine.

What you're trying to do is get 'inside the heads' of your target market.

And to illustrate the point, I'd like you to watch this short video clip:

www.FreeFormulaBook.com/resources

The clip is from the film *What Women Want* starring Mel Gibson and Helen Hunt. The clip starts with Nick (played by Gibson) going to see his shrink, played brilliantly by Bette Midler. The night before, he had an accident, and for some reason he can now 'hear' what women think. It's driving him crazy, and he goes to see Midler for help.

But after reasoning with him, Midler convinces Nick to use his new found 'power', which, of course, he does. It's the final clip where Nick enters the coffee shop that I want you to pay close attention to.

For month's he's been trying to get a date with a barista called Lola (played by Marisa Tomei). Whereas before he went in all guns blazing without thinking about her fears, worries and needs, because he can now hear what she thinks, he can tailor his message (his chat-up lines) to match her worries, which he does.

The results speak for themselves!

That's the power you have when you use target marketing. You can influence people like never before, because you 'get inside their heads' and tailor your message (your chat-up lines) to them.

You must trust me with this.

Do it, and everything else in this book will become 10 times more effective, and your business will be unrecognisable within a few short months.

USING THE SUCCESS FORMULA

$$(I + A + T) = TM$$

(Identify + Avatar + Tailor) = Target Market

Okay. So now you'll use the success formula to create your target market…

(I) IDENTIFY

As we've just discussed, not all customers are created equally, and your business will naturally attract different segments of the market.

The first part of the success formula is to identify those types of customers who are most likely to buy from you.

Look at your existing clients, customers or patients. Which ones are the best? Which ones spend the most money? Are there other segments you could target?

Don't make this more difficult than it needs to be.

(A) AVATAR

Once you've identified your target market(s), you need to build a simple profile of them (the Avatar).

There are **four stages** to this (but don't worry, they're all simple):

STAGE 1: List all common characteristics

I've created a very simple diagram showing the key characteristics you should look for (note there are two diagrams – first for business-to-business, and second for business-to-consumer)...

The Business-to-Business
Target Market Characteristics

Here's a more in-depth look at each characteristic:

- **Industry:**

  What types of businesses do you want to target? Are there some industries that you want to stay clear of? Do you have any specialties with certain industries? Do you have credibility in any industries?

  There are three key factors which influence the selection of the industry:

  1. Your industry experience

     You may want to target industries where you already have experience.

  2. Your industry credibility

     You may want to target industries where you already have credibility.

  3. Your likes and dislikes

     You may have preferences already about industries that you like or dislike. This will obviously have an impact on the choices you make in terms of the industries you select.

- **Decision-Makers:**

  An important consideration is choosing businesses with a simple decision-making process. Clearly, the larger the business, the more likely the number of decision-makers will increase, making the sale more difficult. But it all depends, of course, on what you're selling and to whom!

- **Age of Business:**

  Clearly there is an age range of businesses from start-ups to well-established companies. Are you bothered about how old a business is?

- **Turnover/Number of Employees:**

  Both these demographics are easy indicators for choosing your target market.

  Turnover has a direct impact on the number of decision-makers.

  The Number of Employees is generally linked to turnover; and, again, the greater number of staff, the larger the company is likely to be. It brings in the decision about whether or not to work with sole proprietors!

- **Location:**

  Where exactly do you want your customers to come from? Do not ignore those on your doorstep (a common mistake), as long as they fit in with the other characteristics.

- **Profitability:**

  How concerned are you about working with profitable companies?

Now, let's take a look at the business-to-consumer target market characteristics.

The Business-to-Consumer Target Market Characteristics

Here's a more in-depth look at each characteristic:

- **Accommodation:**

  This refers to the type of dwelling your target market lives in. For example, do most of your customers live in four- or five-bedroom detached homes, or three-bedroom semi-detached? Do they live in apartments or council housing? Do they have large or small gardens, or none at all?

- **Decision-Makers:**

  Is the male or female the main decision-maker, or is it a joint decision (rarely is this the case!).

- **Age:**

  How old are your typical customers? Does it vary depending on gender?

- **Income:**

  What is the combined income of the household? If you're selling high-ticket products or services, this will have a significant bearing on your targeting.

- **Location:**

  Again, where exactly do you want your customers to come from? Do not ignore those on your doorstep (a common mistake), as long as they fit in with the other characteristics.

- **Other Key Demographics:**

  Depending on the type of product or service you sell, there are a multitude of other key demographics that you would want to consider. For example:

  - number of children
  - age of children
  - schools children go to
  - type of employment
  - credit history
  - type of vehicles driven
  - number of credit cards held
  - ethnicity
  - religion
  - and on and on

  You will know what demographics are important to you. Just make sure you factor them in when identifying what the ideal customer 'looks like'.

STAGE 2: Motivations for buying (Psychographics)

Now write down what motivates the decision-makers to buy your product or service. Obviously, if you're selling to consumers rather than businesses, these would be personal specific, but don't forget their motivation may include other people (husband, wife, children, etc.).

If you're selling to businesses, remember you're still selling to people, but that their motivations will be two-fold: personal and business specific.

There are many different motivations for buying. **Here's a list of the 22 main ones:**

1. Addiction: This is outside the range of the normal human operating system, but it certainly exists and accounts for more sales than any of us can fathom. For example, this is the reason the tobacco industry is so huge the world over.

- Affiliation: Something that helps bond you to a cultural, religious or community affiliation.
- Basic Needs: We buy things to fulfil what Maslow describes as the bottom of his hierarchy; things such as food and shelter.
- Celebrity Alignment: People like to have the same things as their favourite celebrity uses. That's why celebrity endorsement works so well.
- Compulsory Purchase: Some external requirement, such as buying school books, uniforms or something required for work, makes it mandatory.
- Convenience: You need something now and will take the easiest or fastest path to get it. Think about the last time you were thirsty and found the nearest type of drink you could. This could also be choosing the safe supplier (no one ever gets fired for hiring IBM), or purchasing something to increase comfort or efficiency.

- Ego Stroking: Sometimes you make a purchase to impress/attract the opposite sex; to have something bigger/better than others, friends, neighbours, etc.; to look like an expert/aficionado; to meet a standard of social status, often exceeding what's realistically affordable to make it at least seem like you operate at a higher level.
- Emergency Purchase: When you need something in an emergency (plumbing, appliance repairs, lock repairs, etc.).
- Empathy: Sometimes people buy from other people because they listened and cared about them even if they had the lesser value alternative.
- Event: When the social decorum of an event (e.g., wedding, anniversary, birthday, etc.) dictates buying something.
- Fear: Many products are purchased out of fear. That doesn't necessarily mean buying things such as household or business alarm systems, it could be fear of loss (the item could sell out), or the product is such an important product to the buyer that they would do anything to get it and would never risk not being able to get it – one of the most powerful motivations.
- Fad or Innovation: Some people (not everyone) want the latest and greatest (it's why each version of the iPhone causes hysteria amongst many).
- Giving: People feel better about themselves by feeling as though they're giving to others, especially when they're promised something in return. Buying things they don't

need – or wouldn't normally purchase – because it will help another person or make the world a better place comes under this category.

- Great Value: When the perceived value substantially exceeds the price of a product or service. This is something you don't particularly need but just feel it's too good a deal to pass up (I'm going to talk more about this later when we discuss *irresistible offers*).
- Indulgence: Who doesn't deserve a bit of luxury now and then? So long as you can afford it (or even if you can't!), sometimes there's no better justification for that hour-long massage, that stunning hand bag or that designer suit.
- Lower Prices: Something you wanted previously but couldn't afford is now cheaper. Maybe you were browsing for a particular handbag or suit, and you saw a great offer.
- Name Recognition: When purchasing a category you're unfamiliar with, branding plays a big role. Think of the first-time purchases you've made over the years and how many of those were influenced by advertising.
- Peer Pressure: Something is purchased because your friends want you to – often happens in teen years.
- Prestige or Aspirational Purchase: Something is bought for an esteem-related reason or for personal enhancement.
- Reciprocity: This happens when somebody, gives or buys you something of value, or does something exceptionally nice and/or unnecessary. Now it's your turn to return the

favour at the next opportunity. This is known as the 'Law Of Reciprocity', and I'll discuss more on this later (it's a very powerful tool).

- Replacement: Sometimes you buy because you need to replace old things you have (e.g., clothes that don't fit or are out of date). This could be moving from a superior model of car, TV, audio system, etc.
- Scarcity: This could be around collectibles or a perceived need that something may run out or have limited availability in the future. Additionally, there's a hope to gain a return on investment, such as collectible or antiques; anything that accrues value over time.

STAGE 3: Key pain points (reasons for buying)

What are their pain points? These are linked to their reasons for buying your product or service. For example, efficiency, ease of use, time, etc.). Write them all down.

STAGE 4: Common Objections (reasons for NOT buying)

What are their most common objections to doing business with you and other people in your specific industry (cost, time, etc.)? Again, write all these down.

By going through this simple four–stage process, you've now built up the ideal profile of your target market. You've got inside their heads, just like Mel Gibson did in *What Women Want*. But this alone isn't going to transform your marketing. What you now need to do is tailor ALL your sales and marketing tactics and strategies to the target market using all the information you've gathered.

(T) TAILOR

As I just mentioned, once you know WHO you're targeting, you can then tailor your sales and marketing strategies to the Avatar Profile.

This is when you connect with the customer or potential customer on a completely different level, and when they say or think, 'this is for ME', your sales and profits will multiply!

The reason is simple: if people see your marketing piece and immediately think 'this is specifically aimed at people like me', then your response rates will immediately increase.

Here are a couple of examples to explain the power of tailoring your message to the target market.

The first example, shown on the next page, is one of my early ads promoting my first-ever business growth system: The POWER Marketing System.

I found there were several particular target markets that were drawn to buying, so naturally I created the Avatar Profile and wrote slightly different ads for each market.

The ad shown was targeted at accountants, but I had slightly different ads for estate agents (realtors), lawyers and printers. The system itself wasn't specifically for accountants, estate agents or lawyers, but the ad appealed to them by getting inside their heads and letting them know I understood their pain, their desires and their requirements.

'ree Report For Accountants Reveals The Secrets Of...

"How To Quickly And Easily Get A Consta 5tream Of New Clients And More Fee Inco From Existing Clients - Guaranteed"

Let's face it, there are just two things which determine your success - getting profitable w clients and generating as much come as you can from your existing ents.

How good you are as an accountant unfortunately not as important. hy would I say this?

Being A Brilliant Accountant Counts For Very Little

Here's the stark reality - even the st Accountant in the world will go oke without a constant stream of w clients and more fee income from isting clients. It's that simple.

The sad **truth** is most people rarely hieve just one of these things, never nd both of them.

The "Secret" Ingredient

It's a familiar story, yet the **key** to ur success is NOT to improve your pertise or even the service levels of ur staff. No. The key is for you to come a sales and marketing **whiz**. at's right you heard me right - And s - you can do it! Here's the **proof**...

'Thanks to your 'secret' sales and narketing approach, we have acquired 76 new clients and are veraging 6 new clients per nonth. This will generate approx £418,000 fee income over the next 5 years. Our average fee income has jumped from £850 to over £1,100."

Rowena Barnwell, Partner
Barnwell Brewin, Ashby

Becoming a sales and marketing pert is a reality I'm sure you're very **ıcomfortable** with. In fact I can ready hear you saying things like, can't do that. I can't do all this stuff d learn about marketing. I just n't see myself ever becoming a arketing genius."

Unfortunately that's what most ople say. And that's why most ople **fail** or never reach their per- nal and business goals.

Heck most accountants don't even e sales and marketing. They think "sell" is a four letter word they'd rather not deal with, and "marketing" is always someone elses job!

Even those that are good at selling don't ever reach their potential because they simply don't have enough prospects to visit. **Why?** Because their marketing isn't churning out a steady supply of prospects who are "desperate" to find the right accountant.

What's The Answer?

What if I said there was a sales and marketing system that once in place runs on **auto-pilot**, and automatical- ly contains the essential and proven business building techniques needed to guarantee your success? Would you be interested?

What if I said this system contained **103** (yes - one - hundred - and - three) different strategies built into it? Every one a critical and important part of what I call the "**success jigsaw**."

Having Sales And Marketing Experience Is Irrelevant

What if I said you needed **no** sales and marketing expertise to create this unbeatable sales and marketing system? You'd be sceptical no doubt, but I'm sure you'd be intrigued.

What if I said this approach has been **100%** successful for every accountant and every other service business provider who has used the system? And the results could be backed up and fully verified. Would you be interested?

How To Guarantee Your Success

I bet you would - even though you may have your reservations. But surely this system doesn't exist does it? **Yes it does!** However, you're prob- ably already doubting much of what I've said. And why wouldn't you?

From time to time we all hear of some hyped up business growth strategy, that turns out to be no better than our worst fears. But I'm not asking you to believe how successful this system is now. All the details are inside my **FREE**

FREE Report Shows You

My **FREE report** title *Profit Secrets: How To Get A Stream Of New Clients And Income From Existing Clie* help. Inside this exciting rep **discover**...

1. The **vital ingredients** th guarantee your success, a to use each one in a simpl powerful growth system
2. How to use the three "**Suc Keys**" to **skyrocket** your and profits
3. The four "**Income Strean Generators**," and using t to catapult your practice f
4. How many of the best and secret practice growth str are actually **FREE** to use identified 67 of them for y
5. How a simple 6 stage "**Sel Without Fear Sales Appointment**" can trans your client acquisitions
6. And **dozens** more secrets

Get Your FREE Cop Right Now

TO GET YOUR FREE (this exciting report, call **recorded message** (24 h [redacted]. Alter complete the coupon and back to me at the address l

Yes! Please send me you FREE Special Report. I to discover the proven growth secrets I can use

First Name: (Mr/Mrs/Ms)
Surname:
Company:
Address:

Tel:
Send To: Hackney Marketing Lt

The ads ran in various industry-specific magazines, and they were very successful.

Remember, even if your product or service isn't specifically for the target market you've identified, you would tailor your message and your product or service to those specific Avatar profiles, so they naturally think 'this is for me'.

For example, let's say you supply customer relationship management (CRM) software to businesses. The software programme isn't tailored to different target markets, but your message to them is. Let's say you identify marketing companies, accountants and health clubs as your target markets. **Whilst your CRM system is identical for each market, their motivations, challenges and reasons for buying (or not buying) are different. You would address these differences in your messages to them.**

The accountant primarily wants it for their existing clients to regularly and easily keep in touch with them to sell more of their services.

The marketing company wants the CRM system to manage their front-end lead-generation campaigns for themselves and their clients.

The health club wants it to manage their membership programme and keep customers motivated to keep coming to the gym.

Your CRM system does all that, but your messages are tailored to the Avatar profiles I've just mentioned, which enables you to connect at a much higher level, because you 'understand' their situation. Consequently, sales increase literally overnight.

The other thing to think about with this is the media you use to deliver your message to the target market.

I'm stating the obvious here, but if you're selling high-value kitchens, for example, that cost tens of thousands of pounds, and you've written an ad specific to your Avatar Profile, there's absolutely no point in placing it in a publication that the more affluent people don't read in their numbers.

Clearly, you'd look for publications that had a readership that in the main fits the profile of your Avatar.

Can you see the power of this?

Yes, it takes more time and effort, but the rewards are significant.

Okay, so the good news is that you've now nailed your target market and created your Avatar Profile.

To make it even easier for you, I've developed a simple Avatar Profile Checklist. You can download it from here:

www.FreeFormulaBook.com/resources

VERY IMPORTANT NOTE: Now you've created your Avatar Profile(s), all the other Core Elements, which I'm going to take you through now, should also be completely focused on each Avatar Profile. This will, of course, maximise your results further.

2. DIFFERENTIATOR

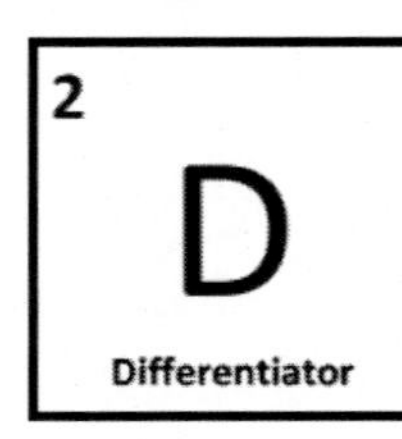

SUCCESS FORMULA:

(U + C + CC) = D

(Uniqueness + Create + Craft and Communicate) = Differentiator

OVERVIEW:

A differentiator is the one thing that sets you apart from the competition. It's WHY customers, clients or patients should choose you over and above anyone else. Communicating this uniqueness is a powerful and persuasive part of each sales and marketing piece you produce.

This is a very weak area for almost every business and one which really hinders growth.

The problem is that customers have become more discerning, which means they're looking for reasons to change or simply use another business: unique reasons; competitive advantages; things that are desirable to them that no other business can offer them.

But because so few businesses create this uniqueness, most people (rightly or wrongly) think ALL businesses are the same within each industry.

So, for example, they think all plumbers are the same, all printers are the same, all furniture stores are the same, and so on. Changing, for the sake of changing, to another supplier who is just going to be like the existing one just isn't worth the hassle. Better the devil you know!

How can you expect your prospects or customers to choose your business over and above any of the competition if they can't quickly see what it is the business does which is so unique and so beneficial to them?

Outstanding businesses have been founded on a differentiator alone. For example, here's a very well-known differentiator:

> 'Red hot pizza delivered to your door
> in 30 minutes or less - guaranteed.'

Tom Monaghan of Domino's Pizza created one of the most successful fast-food franchises in the world based on the strength of this differentiator. It lasted many years until they finally had to remove it because of a couple of fatalities caused by their drivers rushing to deliver the pizzas! But by then, the business was well established.

Just think for a moment about what Tom did.

Notice that he doesn't say, 'the best-tasting pizza'. Domino's pizzas are good, but not the best you can get. No, what he focuses on is what HIS customers (Avatar Profile of the target market) really want.

And his customers (primarily students living within a 5-minute radius of each pizza outlet) often buy on impulse, so they want food delivered quickly, food that is hot!

Sure, they want the pizza to taste good, but they are prepared to 'suffer' a little on quality for hot pizza delivered quickly!

Notice that Tom couldn't have crafted this powerful differentiator if he hadn't known who his target market was. That's why target market has to come before the other Core Elements.

Also notice that a differentiator is NOT about what you do; it's about what you can do for your customers. Find out what your customers want, and then give it to them in a simple and easy-to-understand statement.

Also, understand that when you create a powerful differentiator, it's highly likely that your competition will copy you. But that's okay. You see, as long as you're the first, like Dominos was or the likes of Fed Ex were (guaranteed next-day delivery), this gives you what's known as 'pre-eminence' in your market and is always sufficient to give you the edge you need to rapidly grow your business.

To help you understand this further, I'll tell you a classic story that dates back to 1920s America.

At that time there was an unsuccessful beer company called Schlitz Beer lying a lowly eighth in their market. They went to number 1 in six short months by using a differentiator.

Here's what happened.

At this time there were eight or nine different brewing companies aggressively competing for the same market. Everyone was communicating the same message: that their beer was the purest. They didn't explain what 'pure' meant to the beer drinker, they just kept saying that it was pure, pure, pure. Unfortunately for Schlitz, they were losing ground.

Luckily for them, they were introduced to Claude Hopkins, one of the true legends of marketing. Many of his strategies are still being used today by people like me. Claude asked to be taken around their manufacturing plant.

Like all good marketing people, he wanted as much background information as possible.

As he was being shown around the Schlitz plant, he was amazed at how they made their beer.

First and foremost, their facilities were right at the base of Lake Michigan. Back in the early twenties this water was very pure. Despite this, Schlitz sunk two 5,000-foot-deep artesian wells on the shores because they had to go deep enough to find water the right combination of mineral content to make the best possible beer.

They explained how they went through 1623 different tests and experiments over five years to identify the finest mother yeast cell that could produce the richest taste and flavour. They showed him the intricate water distillation process, in which it was heated to 5,000 degrees Fahrenheit, and then cooled down and condensed. They carried out this process three times to ensure the water was absolutely purified.

They talked about the bottling process where they steamed each bottle at a temperature of 1600 degrees Fahrenheit to kill all bacteria. They finished by telling Claude they had every batch tasted to make sure it was indeed pure and rich before they would even bottle it and send it out the door.

Claude was staggered. The lengths Schlitz went to to purify their beer was amazing. He said to them, 'Why don't you tell people this story?' They replied by saying, 'Everybody goes through this process; it's not unique. It's what must be done to ensure the beer is so pure.'

Claude replied by saying, 'No one knows about this. The first person who tells this story will gain distinction and pre-eminence in their marketplace from then on.'

Schlitz was the first and only beer company that ever told the story of how their beer was formed. It made the word *pure* take on a totally different meaning in the eyes of their prospects and customers, and completely differentiated them from the competition.

The impact was instant and remarkable: a rise to number 1 from number 8 in just six short months. That's the power of a differentiator!

And there are other VERY IMPORTANT factors to consider.

If you are viewed by your customers and prospects as the same as the competition, what do you think becomes the important criterion when customers want your product or service?

That's right: **PRICE**.

There's no hiding the fact that as soon as you create the differentiator for the business, you automatically take the business out of the 'price war' and into the nirvana of higher prices/fees – and less competition! Or – worst case – the same price but the ability to win more custom.

With the advent of the likes of Amazon and their incredible reach and purchasing power, it's so important for you to differentiate your business from everyone else. You must make it as hard as possible for people to compare you with others.

I would say this is the one big thing that holds back many businesses from being very successful.

It's so important that we commissioned our cartoonist to create a cartoon character called Slasher (see next page). It's to make every business owner realise they are competing with this type of business, every single day. He represents all the businesses out there that compete on price and will do anything to get the business, even cutting prices so they make a loss. You have to ensure you position your business out of this slasher-type pricing, and the way to do it is to differentiate.

You should print Slasher out and put him on your desk. It will force you to act on my advice and make sure you eradicate him from being able to have an impact on your business. You can get a copy of 'him' here ...

www.FreeFormulaBook.com/resources

Let's put this to the test.

If I asked you the following question, what would be your answer?

Slasher, a horrible character representing businesses (your competition) that slash and cut prices!

What's the **one unique thing** you offer that makes your prospects think, **'Wow! I must have this product or service'**?

If you're like most people we meet and work with, your answer right now will be, at best, very vague. Few people take the time to articulate what it is they do that is so unique and special for the client or customer.

If you can't accurately describe this uniqueness to your prospects, what chance have they got to find out what you offer over and above the competition?

If the prospect can immediately see **what it is you do that is so unique**, and they find it irresistible, you've created the perfect differentiator.

And remember, your differentiator isn't just about being different from the competition. It's about being different from the competition AND providing something of great benefit to your target market.

To explain this further, I'm going to give you a scenario I've often used with accountants, who, like most other industries, are terrible at differentiating their businesses. Consequently, most compete on price with Slasher firms.

I pick an accountant in the room and say, 'okay I'm going to give you a differentiator that I can guarantee no other accounting firm is offering right now. You're going to be called the Pink Accountants. Everything to do with your firm is pink. Your offices are pink. Your stationery is pink. Your website is pink. Your staff wear pink suits, shirts, blouses and dresses.'

Clearly that's a differentiator, but it's of NO benefit to their clients or prospects, so it's useless. Does that make sense?

A differentiator really is one of the most powerful concepts you can apply to your business, and the good news is that it can be created relatively quickly and easily using the *differentiator success formula...*

$$(U + C + CC) = D$$

(Uniqueness + Create + Craft and Communicate) = Differentiator

(U) UNIQUENESS

Most businesses already have a differentiator; they just don't communicate it, because they forget just how important it is.

Your first task is, therefore, to look over your business (including how you service customers, clients or patients), and your products and services, and identify any differentiator that's already there.

For example, the Tri-Creaser is a device that fits onto the end of folding machines in the printing industry. Although this was an amazing and unique product, for months it was being advertised without highlighting its uniqueness: it completely eliminates fibre-cracking (imperfections when paper and card is folded).

The moment the differentiator was upfront, central and strongly promoted, the business went from doing just a few hundred thousand pounds a year, to millions! That's the difference it can make!

(C) CREATE

Of course, not all businesses have a differentiator. Sometimes you need to create it. There are many ways to do this. Here are 10 proven categories (you'll be able to find one or two that you can tailor to your own business).

1. New and Unique

Sometimes your product is so new and unique that the product itself is the differentiator. Being the original or first mover in the market is a differentiator that nobody can duplicate.

Inevitably, a competitor will emerge with a knock-off or copy of your product, but until then, you can promote the newness and uniqueness of your product as the differentiator.

When the competition heats up, you can switch your differentiator so that it positions your business as the 'first' or 'original' one of its kind.

2. Highest Quality

One well-known brand that immediately comes to mind when you think about quality is the international watch leader Rolex. Rolex also has a short differentiator statement that communicates volumes.

Rolex – 'Quality Takes Time'

3. Expert Status

This type of differentiator communicates the idea that 'I/We am/are the top in my/our field. You can trust my/our knowledge and experience'.

This works well for professionals and other skill- or service-based businesses. Writing a book is one very effective way of positioning you as an expert.

4. Amazing Customer Service

Providing superior customer service is a wonderful way to add value, as well as develop long-term customer loyalty.

To surpass the competition, you must go beyond simply satisfying customers, you have to AMAZE them.

One of the ways to do this is by using *Moments of Truth* (see Chapter 7), whereby you look at every point of contact with your customers and create a WOW experience at each point.

5. The Largest Size/Selection

Providing the largest selection of items can be a powerfully effective differentiator. The classic example of this is Amazon.com. For years (prior to extending their product line) Amazon's differentiator was:

`'Earth's Biggest Bookstore'.`

Amazon.com aren't the only online seller of books, yet it still leads the pack in online bookselling, because they clearly differentiated themselves early on by being the biggest, and as you discovered in the Schlitz Beer example earlier, pre-eminence is an important differentiator.

6. Speed

The speed at which your product or service is delivered can be a powerful differentiator. Offering overnight or second-day shipping as your standard service can give you a strong competitive advantage.

For example, Regus, the serviced office specialists, have a very powerful three-word differentiator that sums up their uniqueness perfectly (quick and everywhere):

`'Instant Offices Worldwide'`

FedEx changed the shipping world when they began guaranteeing overnight delivery of packages. Their differentiator has stood the test of time:

FedEx – 'When It Absolutely Positively Has to Be There Overnight'

7. Strongest Guarantee

A powerful guarantee can immediately give you a compelling differentiator. Guarantee is one of the Core Elements and is discussed shortly.

8. Problem/Solution

Understand that you are not selling a product or service but a major solution to your target market's most pressing problem(s). Remember, having already created your Avatar Profile(s), you'll know what this is. Think about the following situation.

You're out for a business lunch, and someone you've been speaking to asks you this very familiar question:

'What do you do for a living?'

Now, if you were a solicitor/lawyer, a printer or a plumber, you'd probably answer in this way:

'I'm a solicitor.'

'I'm a printer.'

'I'm a plumber.'

These are very common replies and explain why most people 'switch off' after asking this question.

What you must realise is that when you answer in this way regarding your own business, you're saying what you ARE, rather than what you DO FOR YOUR CUSTOMERS!

There's a massive difference.

The good news is that the competition ALSO answer in this way – they don't have a differentiator. All they are selling is the 'product' or the 'service', not the result!

To show you what I mean, let's take the above two examples and add a differentiator.

Solicitor/Lawyer: 'I help people separate within 12 weeks and as amicably as possible.'

Printer: 'I help people sell more of their products or services using innovative and cost-effective printed materials.'

In essence, your differentiator completely focuses on what you do for your specific target market(s). It is the major benefit – the result.

By focusing on the customer's most pressing problems, you can uncover the major benefit.

Think about your prospects' and customers' fears, obstacles and problems. How does your product or service reduce or eliminate these fears? For example, a telemarketing service company would say the major problem their prospects and clients have is:

They can't generate enough leads or enquiries themselves.

Here's how you'd then turn this problem into a powerful benefit.

Problem: They can't generate any leads or enquiries.

Benefit: We help businesses generate high-quality leads.

Do you see how easy this is?

So having identified the major problem your product solves for your chosen target market(s), write the corresponding benefit down.

9. Magic Wand

If your customers and prospects could wave a magic wand over your industry, what would they want most?

Some of the greatest businesses in the world were founded on such thinking. For example, Microsoft was built on this premise:

> 'to make the computer accessible
> and easy to use for everyone'

In an inexpensive way, can you reposition your basic offer in order to meet the customers' major need?

10. THE Biggest, Most Important Benefit

This final method is relatively simple. You need to identify every single feature of your product or service, together with how you operate as a business and how you interact with the customers. Features and Benefits are a Core Element, and I'll be discussing them in detail with you shortly.

However, a good example of this is the Tech-ni-fold Tri-Creaser we mentioned earlier. The major benefit of the Tri-Creaser is that it totally eliminates fibre-cracking. This benefit on its own is so powerful that it became the differentiator. It was further strengthened by adding the word *guaranteed* to it:

'Totally Eliminates Fibre-Cracking - Guaranteed'

To you and me this means very little (unless you're in the printing industry!), but to printers and print finishers, this means everything!

A VERY IMPORTANT NOTE ABOUT USING THE LOWEST PRICE AS THE DIFFERENTIATOR

NEVER, EVER DO IT.

Guaranteeing the lowest price has been used as a differentiator for many businesses (the Slasher firms I alluded to earlier). However, cutting profit margins too deeply is rarely healthy for a business. So, unfortunately, many who have chosen low price as a differentiator are no longer in business. The philosophy is low margins, but high volume.

If your business is small, however, you run the risk of setting off a price war. Larger players in your market who, due to economies of scale, can afford to match or beat your prices in the short-term can easily force you out of the market in the long term. I NEVER recommend setting your stall out to be the cheapest. There is always someone who will undercut you, and being the second-cheapest isn't going to motivate anyone to buy!

(CC) CRAFT AND COMMUNICATE

You should now be left with a fairly short list of options. Now you need to start crafting your differentiator.

Once you've gone through this stage, if you have two or more options you'll quickly be able to determine which differentiator really stands out.

Here are the three rules to define your differentiator:

RULE #1: A short differentiator is more powerful than a long one.

RULE #2: Your differentiator should be clear and easy to understand.

RULE #3: Your differentiator should always focus on your target market.

Take each of your chosen differentiator categories and write down your differentiator. Make sure you adhere to the three rules above.

Having done this, one differentiator should emerge as a clear front runner.

Having spent all this time creating your differentiator, you now need to make sure your clients, customers, or patients and particularly your prospects, know about it. This is critical!

3. HEADLINE

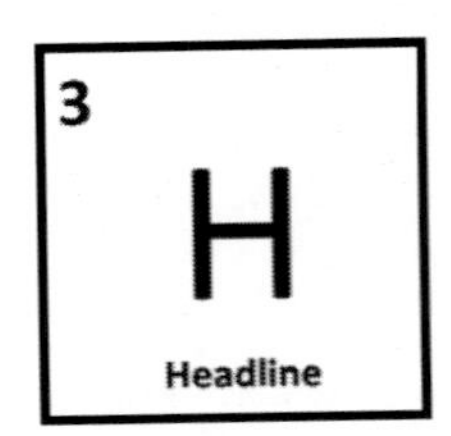

SUCCESS FORMULA:

(HT + T + F) = H

(Headline Template + Test Before Launch + Format) = Headline

OVERVIEW:

Every sales and marketing tactic or strategy you use must include a powerful headline. The name of your business, commonly used as a headline, is NOT a headline!

Headlines are used to grab attention. It should stop the client, customer or patient or prospect dead in their tracks.

A poor headline means no matter how good your message, the target market will simply pass you by.

Think of it like you're waiting for a bus to stop. You can wait by a proper bus stop (the headline), and 99 times out of 100 the bus will stop and let you on. Or you can take your chances and stand anywhere in the street, hold your hand out and hope the bus will stop. You might get lucky five times in every hundred. That's the difference between a good headline and a bad headline.

And like everything else, your headline needs to connect with the target market. So, if your target market is start-ups, then a headline such as...

'Attention Start-Ups: How You Too Can Create A Thriving Business'

...will attract more attention from the target market than a more general headline such as...

'How You Too Can Create A Thriving Business'

When you see it like this, hopefully you can immediately understand why the headline plays such an important role, and why the name of your business really is the worst headline you could ever use!

Think of the headline as the 'ad for the ad'.

If prospects or customers dismiss the headline, that's it; you've lost them. They won't start reading your letter, ad, brochure, website, etc., or listen to your telephone script or radio ad, and you won't get a response or a sale.

To emphasise the importance of headlines, here are a couple of quotes from two of the most highly respected copywriters of all time.

'If you can come up with a good headline, you are almost sure to have a good ad. But even the greatest writer can't save an ad with a poor headline.'

John Caples – *How to Make Your Advertising Make Money*

'On average five times as many people read the headline as read the body copy.'

David Ogilvy – *Confessions of an Advertising Man*

What does this mean? Basically, if you get your headline right, you almost guarantee your success. Get your headline wrong, and your results will suffer!

The image on the next page highlights a simple example to show how few people understand the basic principle of using headlines.

Whilst the Yellow Pages printed directory is extinct, it serves as a great example, because it lists all competing businesses on the same page. Look at the image on the next page. It shows the ads in the category 'Cookers, Stoves & Ovens' – 'Repairs & Spares'. This is typical, and if we did it with websites, for example, we'd have similar results.

Notice the headlines:

Here are the headlines isolated from the ads …

Repairs Specialists

Kingston Appliances

Electric Ovens & Cookers

We Repair or Replace

A1 Cooker Repairs

CT Appliance Repairs

AH Appliance Services

Four of the 'headlines' are the name of the business, and the other three are meaningless. NONE of them grabs the attention. And there's the opportunity.

If all one of those businesses did was to craft a powerful headline, they'd win most of the business in an instant!

Typical 'Headlines' That Don't Work!

Just like in this example, because so many people are doing it wrong, if all you do is lead with a strong headline on all your marketing communications, you'll transform the response and success many times over.

Effective headlines fulfil these four key objectives:

- Get attention.
- Select an audience.
- Deliver a complete message.
- Draw the reader into the body copy (or keep them listening to you, etc.).

The good news is that creating winning headlines can be achieved by following the *headline success formula...*

$$(HT + T + F) = H$$

(Headline Template + Test Before Launch + Format) = Headline

(HT) HEADLINE TEMPLATE

As I said, simply adding a powerful headline to all your marketing pieces will multiply your results.

Many of the headline tests we've carried out over the years have resulted in massive increases in results, and that's testing one great headline against the next.

I've also discovered that there are a number of 'headline templates' which, because of their structure, will always bring results. For example, here's one of my favourites:

How To ...

Simply adding those two words at the start of a headline transforms it into a winner. There are many more. In fact, I've identified 48 of them.

I've listed seven more of my favourites.

By applying these different headline templates, you'll start to see how you can create winning headlines.

To give you an idea of how easy it is to use these templates, I've created a headline for each template based on one of the 'Cooker & Stove' repair ads I showed you earlier.

- **Benefit headlines** (All your headlines should contain a benefit of some sort.)

  My Example:

  `'Same-Day Repair, Or Your Money Back'`

- **Use a two- or three-word headline** (but remember long headlines are almost always more successful then short headlines).

  – Get One Month Free

  – Double Bonus Service

  – Oh My God!

  – Gosh!

  – At Last!

  – Millionaire Secrets

  – If Only ...

My Example:

`'Same-Day Repair'`

- **Headlines that focus on quick and easy solutions**
  - Fast and Simple …
  - Ridiculously Easy and Fast …
  - Idiot-Proof …
  - In Just 10 Days …
  - The 7-Minute Workout …
  - The Lazy Man's Way to …
  - Instant, Automatic Results …
  - The Quick and Easy Way to …

My Example:

`'Your Cooker Repaired Within 24 Hours – Guaranteed'`

- **Warning headlines**
  - Read This Before You …
  - Don't Choose Another Accountant Until You've Read These Facts

My Example:

`'WARNING: Don't Choose Another Cooker Repair Company Until You've Read This'`

- **Testimonial headlines**
  - A Specific Benefit Written Testimonial from One of Your Customers

- "Or It Can Just Be a Headline in Quotation Marks Like This Written Like a Testimonial"

My Example:

"I Called Them at 9.30 a.m., and My Cooker Was Fixed and Working Like New at 3 p.m. the Same Day – Amazing Service"

- **Reasons-why headlines**
  - Seven Reasons Why You Should …
  - 37 Invigorating Reasons …
  - 6 Ways To …
  - 7 Steps …
  - Here's How …

My Example:

'7 Compelling Reasons To Call Us First And Get Your Cooker Repaired The Same Day - Guaranteed'

- **Offer headlines**
  - Put your offer in the headline …
  - Try-Before-You-Buy Accountancy Service

My Example:

'No Call Out Charge And Same-Day Repair, Or Your Money Back'

(T) TEST BEFORE LAUNCH

Next you need to test your headlines.

The ultimate test is, of course, when the tactic or strategy goes live, but it's best to do a test prior to launching, because it can save and make you significant sum of money in the process.

To do this you can use the Pre-Launch Headline Test. I discovered this from Dan Kennedy, the great US marketer.

Very simply, all you do is isolate the headline and add the words: For more information call us on 0800 123 456.

What you then do is score each headline relative to each other on a scale of 1 to 10, with 10 being perfect.

You'll easily be able to pick one or two winners to go with.

(F) FORMAT

Finally, once you've chosen your headline, you need to format it correctly. That depends on where you're using it, and there are several format templates for doing that. As a basic set of guidelines, your headlines should be set in large type, have quotation marks around them and ideally be no longer than 17 words (of the 100 best headlines ever created, based on resulting sales, only five had more than 17 words).

I've created a Headline Creation Template for you to ensure you never worry again about using an under-performing headline.

In fact, this simple document will 'force' you to create highly successful headlines, even if you've never written one in your life before. You can download it from here:

www.FreeFormulaBook.com/resources

4. IRRESISTIBLE OFFER

SUCCESS FORMULA:

(D + S + C) = IO

(Desire + Stimulator + Communicate) = Irresistible Offer

OVERVIEW:

Having an irresistible offer, is absolutely essential when growing your business. So what exactly is it?

It's what your client, customer, patient or prospect gets when they respond to your sales or marketing tactic or strategy. It's created to make it virtually impossible for your target market to resist. Hence, I call it the *irresistible offer*.

The offer is your attempt to get the prospect to stop in their tracks and take action NOW! Therefore, your offer is the inducement to get this response.

As with all the Core Elements, the irresistible offer is once more missing from most marketing I see.

There are two primary types of offers; soft and hard offers. Let's take a look at each.

Soft offers are so named because they don't involve any personal communication with the company making the offer.

As a result, soft offers are the most painless, risk-free way for a prospect to respond. Because of this, and if created correctly, response tends to be high.

I prefer FREE soft offers.

Here is a list of some proven free soft offers:

- free special report
- free brochure
- free catalogue
- free newsletter
- free information pack/kit
- free gift certificate
- free coupon
- free video/video series
- Free Book

These types of soft offers are also known as 'lead magnets', and I will discuss them further in Chapter 5.

Hard offers, on the other hand, require a sale to occur or a personal interaction between the prospect and the seller, or between the prospect and the actual product or service. Here's a list of proven hard offers:

- Free trial
- Free no-obligation appointment
- Free needs assessment audit
- Free explanatory meeting

- Free evaluation of your requirements
- Free initial planning session
- Free executive briefing
- Invitation to a free talk or seminar
- Free use of service
- Free consultation
- Free survey
- Free phone call
- Free analysis
- Free estimate
- Free problem evaluation
- Free demonstration
- The Loss-Leader Offer

I just want to spend a little time talking about 'loss-leader offers'. If customers make more than one purchase (buying print, accountancy services, legal services, or almost every other type of business) you may not need to make a profit on the first order.

That's why you often see the following offers: 27-piece luggage sets for £29.95, 4 Books for £4.00, etc.

This type of offer was pioneered in the 1920s by a marketing genius called Maxwell Sackheim when he created the American Book Club. Many book clubs have copied this approach since, but you can apply it to your business, too.

On the next page there's a more recent example...

Clearly, the book club (or music club, etc.) is losing money on the first sale, but the offer is so compelling that it forces many people to join. Here's a similar offer from the Daily Telegraph (a UK daily broadsheet newspaper), which is equally impressive...

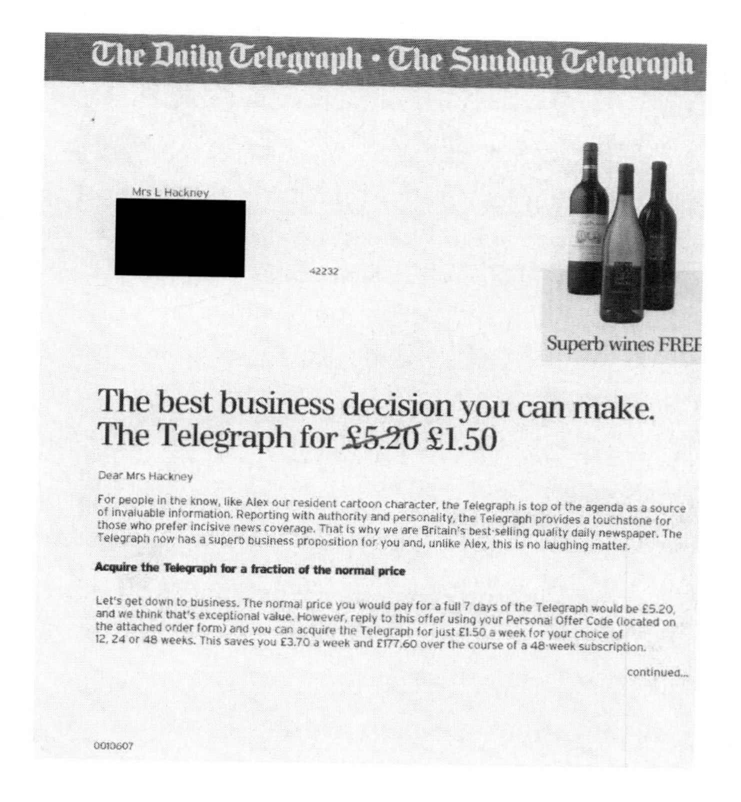

The Daily Telegraph • The Sunday Telegraph

Mrs L Hackney

42232

Superb wines FREE

The best business decision you can make. The Telegraph for ~~£5.20~~ £1.50

Dear Mrs Hackney

For people in the know, like Alex our resident cartoon character, the Telegraph is top of the agenda as a source of invaluable information. Reporting with authority and personality, the Telegraph provides a touchstone for those who prefer incisive news coverage. That is why we are Britain's best-selling quality daily newspaper. The Telegraph now has a superb business proposition for you and, unlike Alex, this is no laughing matter.

Acquire the Telegraph for a fraction of the normal price

Let's get down to business. The normal price you would pay for a full 7 days of the Telegraph would be £5.20, and we think that's exceptional value. However, reply to this offer using your Personal Offer Code (located on the attached order form) and you can acquire the Telegraph for just £1.50 a week for your choice of 12, 24 or 48 weeks. This saves you £3.70 a week and £177.60 over the course of a 48-week subscription.

continued...

0010607

Before I take you through the success formula, I want to highlight another big mistake businesses make: they base all their results on the first sale. Here's what I mean.

Let's say on the first sale a new customer pays you £1,000. Your gross margin after delivering the product or service is 50%, which means you make £500 per new customer.

However, it costs you £600 to generate this one customer (the cost of advertising), so you actually made a loss of £100. Based on these assumptions, you'd conclude that this approach was not profitable, and you may cease to use it.

That's how 99% of business people evaluate their success – based on the first transaction or sale. Do you think the book clubs view their customers like this?

In most businesses the customer keeps coming back for more. And even if you sell a 'one-off' product or service, you can and should get referrals from the customers, and you MUST start looking to 'partner' with other non-competing but aligned businesses so you can offer their products or services (for a commission, of course!).

That means the customer is actually worth much more to you than the amount generated on the first transaction.

This, in effect, is what's known as 'lifetime customer value'.

Quite simply, lifetime customer value is the total profit an average customer generates during the lifetime of the relationship with the business.

Working out lifetime customer value

Before looking at irresistible offers, you need to work out the lifetime customer value of your customers.

Let's say one new customer generates £1,000 per year for five years, and that your gross margin is 50%. That means the average lifetime value over five years is £2,500. Note also that this figure doesn't include referrals (see Chapter 7), which you should also factor in.

Now let's say you currently use Google Ads as one of your lead-generation tactics to generate new customers, and you generate one customer from 100 clicks that cost £200.

This means your cost of acquisition using Google Ads is £200. If you get two customers from the above scenario, the cost of acquisition would be £100, and so on.

This means you're left with £2,300 (the gross profit minus your cost of acquisition). That's pretty good.

Here's how you can use this in your favour. Listen up, because this will have a huge impact on the business.

First, if you know that every £200 you spend to generate a new customer, results in new profit of £2,300, you should do more of it – much more!

Second, in the example above you should test your Ads campaign, making sure you're taking full advantage of the Core Elements, and only small improvements will result in bigger returns for you, for no extra spend.

And finally, the key to success is that now you know how much a customer is worth, you can spend more to acquire them in the first place (an even more irresistible offer).

Now, clearly, there are a few things you need to consider before creating an irresistible offer.

The irresistible offers you create make it impossible for your prospects to ignore you, and, as a result, your sales increase rapidly!

Just to whet your appetite, below is an irresistible offer (and the full letter) that catapulted the outside catering sales for a new franchise food outlet, from sales of £0 a week to over £6,000 a week in less than three months!

This was the offer sent to businesses operating within a one-mile radius of the store. The companies targeted were large organisations, which have a greater need for outside catering (Avatar Profile).

Because we knew these organisations would be ordering frequently, we were confident that if we could get them to sample the food and service, we'd secure their business.

And that's just what happened (study this letter carefully. There's much to be gained from this approach)!

'Are You Planning a Business Meeting That Requires Fresh High-Quality Food at a Very Reasonable Price?'

'Order Your FREE O'Briens Five-Star Sandwich Platter'

Dear <Name>

Here's the deal …

You can receive a delicious O'Briens Five-Star Sandwich Platter (serves five people) - totally FREE. Or you can deduct the cost from your first order.

I'm not talking about your standard 'buffet' food. I'm talking about high-quality food made daily from fresh produce. I'm talking about presentation and packaging that makes an instant impact on people. Perfect for any meeting or special occasion with staff, associates or Clients/Customers.

So why am I doing this?

Quite simply, I've found that as soon as people taste our food and see our presentation and packaging, they're hooked. Nothing compares to this. They love it! And I've learned that by providing a free platter we stand a better chance of getting your business in the long run.

I suppose the 'proof of the pudding is in the eating'. You can instantly form your own impression, having sampled our food. And that's it. No strings. No obligation.

Frankly, our platters are not for everyone. If you're not concerned about the impact your food has on your staff, associates and Clients/Customers, then we aren't for you. If, on the other hand, you truly appreciate the importance of having superbly presented high-quality food and the positive impact this creates, then I urge you to call our FREEPHONE Platter Hotline on <Number>.

So what's the catch?

Well there isn't one - as long as you respond quickly. Clearly I can't keep this offer open indefinitely. You must reply before Friday 6th July to get your FREE Five-Star Platter. So the quicker you reply, the less likely you are to be disappointed!

Why should you even try us out?

I appreciate the offer of a 'free lunch' may not be enough to persuade you to place your order. After all, I know how important your meetings can be. However, I consider ourselves the only specialist caterers for the business market in Leicester. Sure, other companies do it - but have they really thought about your real needs and wants? For example, do they offer …

- A guarantee to deliver on time …

  Guarantee 1: We will deliver your entire order on time, or you don't pay us a single penny.

  Guarantee 2: If we do deliver your order late, your next meal is FREE (to the same value as your original order).

- A varied and delicious menu with 10 choices of bread, choice of drinks (hot or cold), and catering for vegetarians

- An instant meal where the food arrives ready for presentation on your tables

- Catering for 5 to 5,000 people

We offer all this as 'standard'. How many people do you think would be willing to offer such a guarantee? But that's the point. We guarantee on-time delivery because we know how important this is to you. If we fail, we suffer - not you. Isn't that how it should be?

In fact, read the enclosed customer testimonials - you'll see our customers rave about our catering services.

I'm sure you can now appreciate why I think you should take advantage of my FREE offer. Do it now. Call our FREEPHONE Platter Hotline on <Number>. We are eagerly awaiting your call.

Kind regards

<Name>

Managing Director

P.S. Don't delay. This offer is only available until July 6th. Call me now on our FREEPHONE Platter Hotline on <Number>. Thank you.

P.P.S. FREE DELIVERY! Whether your meeting is early in the morning, at lunchtime, or in the evening, we will deliver to you FREE of charge!

Do you see the power of using loss-leaders? Do you now see the significant shift in thinking you've just taken?

You've gone from

How much money did we make on the first order?

to

How much money will we make over the duration of the relationship?

This is a massive difference!

Attracting loyal customers of the competition to you

When you get the irresistible offer right, you'll also attract customers from your competitors. Even the most loyal customers can be tempted with the right offer.

Remember, an irresistible offer can overcome even long-term relationships, relationships you once thought were impregnable. Here's a very good example. The short letter shown below (printed word for word) was sent by the prep school my children went to...

> **Change of Book Club**
>
> Baker Books have offered us a special introductory offer of free books to the value of our summer order from their pupil book club catalogues.
>
> In other words, if the value of the order is £600, we will receive £600 worth of free books for school. This is too good an offer to refuse and so we will be changing to the BAKER BOOK CLUB. I would be grateful for your support.
>
> Yours sincerely,
> Jenny Read

As you can see, the school is letting all the parents know they've decided to change book club companies. After receiving this letter, I asked the school how long they had been with the existing book club, and they'd been with them for 15 years!

Take a look at paragraph two. This is what your offer needs to achieve:

```
'This is too good an offer to refuse
and so we will be changing to the BAKER BOOK CLUB'
```

In this example, Baker Books have created such an irresistible offer that the school simply couldn't refuse – even though they had a longstanding relationship with the incumbent book club. Can you see just how powerful this marketing technique can be? And I'd guess many other schools have acted in a similar way.

What Baker Books have done is, first, realise the lifetime customer value of their customers (the schools). Second, they've figured out what they can afford to spend to get a customer (i.e. match the first order with the same amount of free books for the school). Very simple, but very effective.

But don't forget there's a double-edged sword to this:

If you can win new customers with irresistible offers, your own customers are open to offers from their competitors.

The key, once you've won the business, is to add so much value that the customer never wants to leave, irrespective of the offers that come their way (see Chapter 7)!

Okay. Let's now take a look at the success formula...

$$(D + S + C) = IO$$

(Desire + Stimulator + Communicate) = Irresistible Offer

(D) DESIRE

As I've just discussed, the key to creating an irresistible offer is being able to offer something to your potential or existing customers that they highly desire.

I've given you many examples. As always, the key is to look at your Avatar Profile and think: what would be highly desirable to them?

(S) STIMULATOR

Once you've got an irresistible offer, you need to do everything in your power to get people to take action, and take it NOW!

That's why you need a 'stimulator'. It reduces procrastination.

For example, you can use deadlines, limited availability, etc.

(C) COMMUNICATE

Once you've created your irresistible offer, you need to communicate it on all your relevant sales and marketing tactics and strategies.

Once again, to make this whole process even easier for you, I've created an *Irresistible Offer Checklist*, which you can download from here:

www.FreeFormulaBook.com/resources

5. FEATURES AND BENEFITS

SUCCESS FORMULA:

(FL + L + CB + OI) = FAB

(Feature List + Link + Craft Benefit + Order Of Importance) = Features & Benefits

OVERVIEW:

Almost every business owner is aware of features and benefits. But it's surprising how few people actually use benefits in their sales and marketing.

All too often the features are communicated rather than the more powerful corresponding benefits. As a result, the power of your marketing is reduced significantly.

When you try to sell the features of your product or service, you're making the customer do all the work to figure out why they want the feature. It's in a seller's best interest to draw the connection for them. But to do that, you have to know and articulate the results (benefits) yourself.

Benefits are the 'sizzle'; they are the emotional triggers that help in the decision-making process. Elmer Wheeler, the famous sales trainer in the USA, said it perfectly: **'sell the sizzle, not the steak'**.

A feature (the steak) is a statement of what you do or what something does. It forms the logical part of a decision-making process.

Therefore, both features (the steak) AND benefits (the sizzle) are important.

Here's the success formula…

$$(FL + L + CB + OI) = FAB$$

(Feature List + Link + Craft Benefit + Order Of Importance) = Features & Benefits

(FL) FEATURE LIST

First, you need to write a list of all the features of your product or service – all of them. Using a very simple example, let's say your product is a hole punch. These are some of the features you'd write down:

- made of hardened steel
- plastic cover on the base
- removable base
- plastic guide for your paper

(L) LINK

Then, to make the process of writing the corresponding benefits easier, use what's called a 'link'. Next to each feature write the words 'which means that'.

(CB) CRAFT BENEFIT

Now create the corresponding benefit.

I'll be honest with you, the first time you do this, you'll find it a challenge. But believe me it's worth the time and effort.

For example, here are three features:

- self-setting clock
- open 24 hours
- batteries included

Each is a feature, a factual statement about the product or service being promoted.

Let's look at the corresponding benefits of the features above.

- The benefit of a self-setting clock is convenience.
- The benefit of a store open 24 hours is that you can buy when you want.
- The benefit of batteries included is that the product is ready to use out of the box.

Whilst these may seem like true benefits, we can go further. You should view your benefits as **'results'**.

The best way to understand the true benefit of your product or service is to answer the **'What's in it for me?'** question and to focus on results.

Let's take another look at that features list to see the possible benefits from the customer's point of view.

- Self-setting clock: I won't feel dumb!
- Open 24 hours: When my pregnant wife craves ice cream at 4 a.m., I won't have to disappoint her.
- Batteries included: I'll never have to see the crushed look on my child's face when his toy won't work because I forgot to buy batteries.

See the difference?

(OI) ORDER OF IMPORTANCE

Finally, put your benefits in order of importance: biggest first, second-biggest next, and so on. Use them in this order!

A big mistake is that people think they should build to a 'crescendo'. But tests have proved that you should start with your biggest benefit, and so on.

6. GUARANTEE

SUCCESS FORMULA:

(GP + P) = G

(Guarantee The Promise + Punish The Business If Promise Not Delivered) = Guarantee

OVERVIEW:

My experience tells me that fewer than one in 100,000 small or medium sized businesses actually use a guarantee in their business. This is a BIG mistake.

A guarantee works at the point of purchase and is what I call a **'sales converter'** (discussed again in Chapter 6).

Therefore, applying a guarantee will increase sales immediately. Yes instantly!

Why do guarantees work so well?

As you know, the benefit of your product or service is gained after the sale is made – after you've acquired the customer. Sometimes this can be days, weeks, months or even years after the first sale was made (depending on what you sell).

This in itself places a risk on the shoulders of would-be customers. It's this risk that often prevents them from buying or changing suppliers, even though they're not happy.

However, if you lower or eliminate this risk, then the natural consequence is people will be more inclined to buy from you. Agreed?

That's the secret of creating a powerful guarantee that mitigates against the risk.

A guarantee is nothing more than simply taking away the barriers from the sale and ensures that the prospect keeps progressing towards the sale.

As soon as you add a guarantee it removes the risks of buying, ensuring more clients, customers or patients are gained. It automatically differentiates the business from the competition, and it adds value.

Prospects will value your services much more, because they'll assume the service must live up to expectations, and the business must be excellent at delivering the service. ('Why would they offer a guarantee if the product or service wasn't great?').

The result is therefore a **BIG increase in new customers**!

The ultimate aim is to guarantee the result or main benefit of your service and add a 'penalty' should the service fail to live up to your promises.

Just to explain this further, here's a simple example of how risk reversal works. A man wants to buy a puppy for his daughter. He responds to two ads in the local newsagent's window. He examines the first puppy, and it seems ideal in temperament and looks. The owner says to the man, 'If the dog isn't right for your daughter, bring it back in a week, and I'll give you your money back.' Clearly, he appreciated the value of risk reversal and guarantees, but he didn't fully understand it!

The man then goes to look at the second puppy. Again, it seems ideal in temperament and looks. Only this time the owner says, 'Your daughter is obviously looking forward to her new puppy, and it's important that she's totally happy with it. Please take the puppy, let your daughter play with it, look after it, and get to know it. If after three weeks the puppy is not right for her, bring the puppy back, and I'll refund your money in full and give you £50 for your time, effort and trouble.'

Now this man really understands risk reversal. First, he extended the 'trial' period. He knows that his puppy is a good dog. He also knows that after three weeks the puppy and girl will be inseparable. He totally reverses the risk.

You also need to understand this. The company that reverses the risk automatically gains a competitive advantage and wins more business – in fact, much more! This competitive advantage is very significant when attracting new customers to your business.

Here's another example, one of the best I've ever seen. It's from a pest control company called BBBK. Their guarantee is aimed at hotels and restaurants., Just pretend, for a second, that you're a restaurateur and you have a problem with rodents. You're looking for a pest control company, and you see the following guarantee:

> You don't owe one penny until all the pests on your premises have been eradicated.
>
> If you are ever dissatisfied with BBBK's services you will receive a refund for up to 12 months of the company's services … plus fees for another exterminator of your choice for the next year.
>
> If a guest spots a pest on your premises, BBBK will pay for the guest's meal or room, send a letter of apology, and pay for a future meal or stay … and if your facility is closed down due to the presence of roaches or rodents, BBBK will pay any fines, as well as all lost profits, plus $5,000.

I defy you not to at least call them to find out more!

Although I don't know for certain, it's easy to assume several things about BBBK from this guarantee.

They are very good at pest control.

They understand the concerns of their customers with regard to hygiene and the potentially damaging effects of any infestation.

They are very successful at attracting new customers!

They are probably providing very similar services to their competitors. However, they understand risk reversal and guarantees. Their profits, I'm sure, will reflect this!

Hopefully you now have a basic grasp of guarantees and what they can achieve for your business. However, several questions may be entering your mind.

For example, 'Won't people try to abuse what I am offering?' and 'Won't I lose a lot of money with this?'

The key, of course, to successful guarantees is this: if you offer a good product or service (which you do), then you have nothing to worry about.

And ...

ONLY GUARANTEE WHAT YOU CONTROL.

If you do that, you'll never have to worry about your guarantee, although I can't promise that no one will take advantage of it. But the way to look at it is that it will be a very small minority who do take advantage, and the increase in sales will far outweigh any refunds you have to give.

Therefore, you should be thinking about guaranteeing the results your products or services provide; guaranteeing delivery times on work; guaranteeing support services – you name it. Whatever you do and how you do it, you can guarantee it, and the bolder you are, the better.

One last point to mention is about adding 'conditions'. You should avoid adding conditions to the guarantee, otherwise the guarantee is weakened. If the condition is 'fair enough', such as 'normal wear and tear', then fine, add it, but just remember conditions can sometimes make the guarantee virtually obsolete or worthless.

Let's now look at the success formula...

(GP + P) = G

(Guarantee The Promise + Punish The Business If Promise Not Delivered) = Guarantee

(GP) GUARANTEE THE PROMISE

The first thing you need to do is 'guarantee the promise'. In other words, identify the ultimate result that the customer is buying, and then promise you will deliver on it.

For example, referring back to the differentiator Domino's Pizza used:

> 'Red hot pizza delivered to your door
> in 30 minutes or less guaranteed'

Notice they guarantee the promise, which is to deliver 'red hot pizza in 30 minutes or less'.

(P) PUNISH THE BUSINESS IF PROMISE NOT DELIVERED

When you apply the first part of the success formula, it will immediately translate into sales. However, by adding this second part, your sales will increase even further.

What you need to do is 'punish' the business if it doesn't deliver the promised results.

For example, if Dominos don't deliver your pizza within 30 minutes, it's FREE.

If BBBK foul up, they refund the fees and pay for another exterminator, etc.

Be bold. Remember, if you're only guaranteeing what you control, you can be really confident! It will translate into many more sales.

7. REASONS WHY

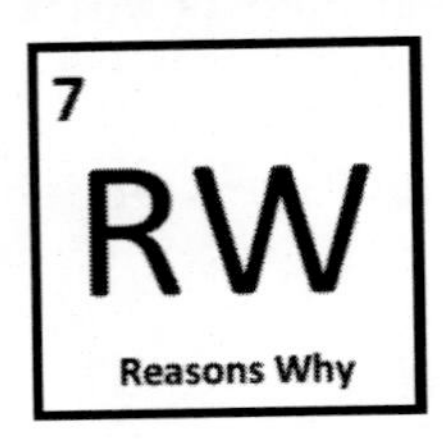

SUCCESS FORMULA:

(R + A) = RW

(Rationale + Articulate) = Reasons Why

OVERVIEW:

When you use a sensational guarantee or an irresistible offer, or you make a statement that could be hard to believe, then if you don't back them up with reasons why, you'll lose sales, because people will think 'it's too good to be true'.

The more sensational the offer or guarantee, the more reasons you need to back it up with.

Therefore, you use 'reasons why' to validate and make your message sound believable.

This is actually very easy to apply. All you do is explain in simple terms why you offer your guarantee or why you have an amazing offer.

Be honest.

There's no need to make it up.

For example, here's the guarantee for an estate agent:

'If we don't sell your house within a week for the price we agree, we'll give you £500.'

Here's the 'reasons why', word for word:

'Why would we do this?

'It's quite simple really. Last year we sold 1,817 houses – more than any other estate agent in Leicestershire. We're very good at it (read our testimonials).

'But since you've never used us before to sell your home, we wanted to give you something that would put your mind at rest and reassure you that we can deliver (over-deliver) on our promises. That's why we offer this fantastic guarantee.'

Do you see what we're doing here? The 'reasons why' actually support and validate the guarantee, and makes it believable!

Let's look at the success formula…

(R + A) = RW

(Rationale + Articulate) = Reasons Why

(R) RATIONALE

The best way to think about this is that you just need to justify WHY you're doing it or saying it.

For example, you could be the quickest at delivering X. If that's the case, you need to explain WHY you're the quickest at delivering X. Adding the rationale behind why you're the quickest makes it believable and, in fact, adds even more sales power.

Here's another example – it's the guarantee we offer with our coaching programmes.

Join with Complete Peace of Mind with Our 90-Day, No Questions Asked, Money-Back GUARANTEE

(A) ARTICULATE

You then simply need to articulate the rationale so it makes sense and completely overcomes any cynicism or doubts in the mind of your customer or potential customer.

And here are the reasons why.

All we're really asking you to say is 'maybe'. Don't risk a single penny or cent with our unconditional 90-day money-back GUARANTEE.

The guarantee is in place to give you complete peace of mind. We know how good our coaching programmes are, and the guarantee shows we stand by them 100%.

Join today, and if within the first 90 days, for any reason, you want to cancel, simply let us know, and we'll refund every single penny you've paid. We can't be fairer than that!

8. SOCIAL PROOF

SUCCESS FORMULA:

(CB + C) = SP

(Credibility Builders + Communicate) = Social Proof

OVERVIEW:

What further supports your message and proves that you do deliver on your promises is the use of something that's known as *social proof*.

Social proof is a term used to describe a set of credibility builders. The more credibility you have in your sales and marketing, the more believable it all becomes, and that instantly translates into transformed results.

Credibility builders include

- comments and testimonials from clients, customers or patients
- case studies
- membership of credible associations
- industry awards, etc.

The more you include, the better.

Once again, the more aligned to your target market(s), the more powerful your social proof will be.

For example, if your target market is businesses who turnover £250k to £500k, the only testimonials you should be using are from businesses of a similar size.

If you sell to the affluent, then your case studies should be from affluent customers salivating over your product or service.

I cannot overstate the importance of this. Relevance is a key motivator, so the more relevant your social media (and everything else!) is to the target market, the more appealing you'll become to them.

Think about your own purchasing decisions. Isn't it more comforting to know people are pleased with their experience with the business selling the product or service.

How often do you book a holiday or hotel without looking at the reviews from customers? How influential is a bad comment and, conversely, a good comment?

Review sites are becoming more and more important, and 'Reputation Marketing' (as it's now called) is playing a significant role, especially online, in purchasing decisions. That's social proof.

As you can see, testimonials play a big part in convincing your target market that others have tried your product and service, and that they have had a good experience.

Ideally, your testimonials should stress a number of your key benefits. The more positive the reinforcement of your overall offer, the better.

You may think getting customer testimonials is challenging. It's not. Simply write to the relevant customers and ask them to give you a few comments about what they like about your business, and ask for their permission to use their comments on your material. You'll be surprised at the responses you get and how good the comments are.

Then, once you've got your supply of testimonials, simply use the ones which convey your benefits best. It really is that simple!

Let's take a look at the success formula...

(CB + C) = SP

(Credibility Builders + Communicate) = Social Proof

(CB) CREDIBILITY BUILDERS

Your task here is simple. Create and develop as many credibility builders (listed above). As I said, the more, the better.

(C) COMMUNICATE

Once you've collected your credibility builders, you need to then add them and communicate them in your sales and marketing tactics and strategies.

9. CALL TO ACTION

SUCCESS FORMULA:

(SO + SR + MR + WHN) = CTA

(Summarise The Offer + Stimulator Reminder + Multiple Ways Of Responding + What Happens Next) = Call To Action

OVERVIEW:

And finally, in all your sales and marketing tactics and strategies you use a powerful call to action. Remember, the purpose of every marketing piece is simple: you must get the recipient to act, and you must get them to act now!

Getting anyone to DO something isn't easy. More often than not, the prospect or customer is busy. Other things are demanding their attention. In fact, responding is usually not convenient and they need to be pushed to take action.

The late, great copywriter Gary Halbert said, 'you should pretend your prospect is a huge sloth of a man sitting in his chair'.

To get him to move one inch requires enormous effort. Your sales and marketing must be powerful enough to get him out of his comfortable seat and respond.

It's very easy for your prospect to say to themselves, 'I'll reply tomorrow.' But, as we all know, tomorrow often never comes!

Therefore, your number-one goal is to get a response now.

Your call to action is all-important in achieving this objective. Tests have proved that without a call to action your sales and marketing is likely to be 50% less effective – that's how important the call to action is.

Yet it's missing from most sales and marketing tactics and strategies. A call to action isn't just adding your phone number to the bottom or top of your website, or adding your website URL at the bottom of a letter.

You literally have to tell your recipient what to do next.

Again, this is very simple to do.

If you want them to go to your website, you'd say something like this:

Simply click on this link, and you'll go straight to our website. From there, you can immediately download our FREE special report titled, 'How to Create a Thick, Lush Green Lawn 12 Months of the Year'. Remember, the report is FREE until 13 June, so go and get it now.

Do you see how easy this is?

Let's put it all together with the success formula...

(SO + SR + MR +WHN) = CTA

(Summarise The Offer + Stimulator Reminder + Multiple Ways Of Responding + What Happens Next) = Call To Action

(SO) SUMMARISE THE OFFER

The first thing you need to do is to Summarise The Offer. Tell them what they will get when they respond.

For example:

To download our FREE special report detailing the 'Seven Secrets to Saving Five Figures in Tax' …

(SR) STIMULATOR REMINDER

Next, remind them why they need to respond now (your 'Stimulator'):

Remember, download our FREE special report detailing the 'Seven Secrets to Saving Five Figures in Tax' within the next four days …

(MR) MULTIPLE WAYS OF RESPONDING

Then, give them more than one way to respond (unless you have good reason for offering just one way of responding). People have preferential ways of responding and buying. The more options you give, the better your results will be.

Remember, download our FREE special report detailing the 'Seven Secrets to Saving Five Figures in Tax' within the next four days. Simply go to www.abc.com or call us on 0800 123 456 …

(WHN) WHAT HAPPENS NEXT

Finally, tell them what will happen when they respond.

Remember, download our FREE special report detailing the 'Seven Secrets to Saving Five Figures in Tax' within the next four days. Simply go to www.abc.com, or call us on 0800 123 456. You'll then be able to `apply each of the strategies and secrets to your own business, resulting in huge savings in tax. Do it now.`

***

Okay. Those are the nine Core Elements. I promise that as soon as you start applying them to all your sales and marketing tactics and strategies, you'll see a remarkable and instant uplift in results.

Remember, adding or improving each of the Core Elements doesn't cost you a single penny. You're using the Core Elements to make your sales and marketing work more effectively.

Go through all your existing tactics and strategies and, one-by-one, add the Core Elements to them.

Then, when you add any new tactics or strategies, make sure the Core Elements are included in them.

It's impossible NOT to transform your results when you do this.

You're on your way now. You now know what makes marketing work and what's required to get results.

That's the first part of THE FORMULA ...

$$(T \times L \times C \times M)S$$

Next, we're going to look at the tactics and strategies you're going to use across the 'L', 'C' and 'M' parts of THE FORMULA, but first I want to explain why I'm recommending you use these strategies, and why I guarantee they'll work for you.

Chapter Summary

- Marketing is your ability to influence people to buy your products or services.
- The 9 'Core Elements' are the Marketing DNA... the things that make marketing work.
- You'll transform the results of your sales and marketing when you apply them to your tactics and strategies.
- 9 Core Elements...

1. **Target Market:**
   Success Formula: (I + A + T) = TM
   (Identity + Avatar + Tailor) = Target Market

2. **Differentiator:**
   Success Formula: (U + C + CC) = D
   (Unique + Create Uniqueness+ Craft & Communicate) = Differentiator

3. **Headline:**
   Success Formula: (HT + T + F) = H
   (Headline Template + Test Before Launch + Format) = Headline

4. **Irresistible Offer:**
   Success Formula: (D + S + C) = IO
   (Desire + Stimulator + Communicate) = Irresistible Offer

5. **Features & Benefits:**
   Success Formula: (FL + L + CB + OI) = FAB
   (Feature List + Link + Craft Benefit + Order of Importance) = Features and Benefits

6. **Guarantee:**
   Success Formula: (GP + P) = G
   (Guarantee the Promise + Punish The Business If Promise Not Delivered) = Guarantee

7. **Reasons Why:**
   Success Formula: (R + A) = RW
   (Rationale + Articulate) = Reasons Why

8. **Social Proof:**
   Success Formula: (CB + C) = SP
   (Credibility Builders + Communicate) = Social Proof

9. **Call To Action**:
   Success Formula: (SO + SR + MR + WHN) = CTA
   (Summarise The Offer + Stimulator Reminder + Multiple Ways of Responding + What Happens Next) = Call To Action

CHAPTER 4:

THE WORLD'S MOST SUCCESSFUL SALES AND MARKETING STRATEGIES FOR ANY BUSINESS

As you know, there are hundreds, if not thousands, of different sales and marketing tactics and strategies available to a business owner. Therefore, your challenge is choosing the ones that are going to give you the best return on investment in the shortest time possible with the minimum time spent implementing them. Correct?

Well, that's what this short chapter is about. Before taking you through the specific tactics and strategies for each of the component parts of THE FORMULA, I want to share with you WHY I recommend you use the strategies and tactics in each chapter.

Believe me, this is a minefield. You can end up being a busy fool, or, worse still, you can literally lose the shirt off your back if you use the wrong strategies for your business.

I've seen it happen many, many times.

In fact, here's a true story to reinforce the point.

Several years ago, my accountant recommended me to a Web design company. They had been running six months and were struggling.

I met the owner of the business and asked him to give me a summary of what he'd done in his first six months.

Surprisingly, he was well invested (I say 'surprisingly' because most businesses start on a shoestring). He had £30,000 from savings as capital. That was the only bit of good news.

He'd been seduced by the local newspaper, which had a readership of a couple of hundred thousand, and had agreed to take out an ad programme with them over six months. Total cost £18,000!

Guess how many leads and customers the ads generated?

ZERO.

Not a single lead or customer.

£18,000 down the pan.

Now you probably haven't lost that kind of money on an ad campaign, but the point I'm trying to make is that it's easy to lose money with poor choices.

You're already in a better position than most, because you now know how to make your sales and marketing effective by using the Core Elements, but unless you've tried, tested and proved a particular tactic or strategy, how do you know it's going to work for you?

Well, that's basically what I've done for you. Naturally, we haven't tested every single sales and marketing tactic or strategy in existence, but I do know which ones work for 99% of businesses as long as they are applied correctly.

And, as I said in the Introduction, these are timeless strategies that will keep working for you for months and years.

Plus, you also need to understand the power of THE FORMULA and what you now have in your grasp.

You just need to use several well-chosen strategies across each component of THE FORMULA, and you'll automatically build your business exponentially.

I'm therefore going to give you a choice of my favourite tactics and strategies. These are the ones we use day in, day out and, more importantly, more than 26,000 businesses are also using them to grow their businesses quickly.

Here's why they 'make the cut':

- **PROVEN:** You want to know with complete certainty that as long as you apply the tactics and strategies correctly, you're going to get results. Everything in these pages has been proven, not once, but many, many times over. You can be confident that they will work for you, too.

- **UNIVERSAL:** No matter what business you run, you want to know that they will work for you, so the strategies I've included in this book, just like the Core Elements, have universal application.

- **QUICK:** There are tactics and strategies that take time to develop. For example, building a social media presence and keeping everything up to date and fresh is a daily commitment (drag!). I'm not saying you shouldn't use social media, and as long as you apply the Core Elements to it, it will be successful, but it's not for this book. My mantra for you is simple: I give you tactics and strategies that you can implement quickly – within a few hours or days, <u>not</u> weeks or months.

- **EASY TO IMPLEMENT:** Without question, there are strategies I use and recommend that are complex. For example, we use 'Launch Sequences', which are very successful but are often highly complex and require an enormous amount of thinking and time to put in place. So again, whilst I do advocate using launches and other complex strategies, they're not in this book.

- **LONG-LASTING:** You also want tactics and strategies which **stand the test of time**. You don't want to apply a strategy only for it to stop working or be redundant after a couple of weeks or months. Minimal effort for maximum results over a long period of time is what you want.

- **COST-EFFECTIVE:** And last but not least, all the tactics and strategies I recommend in this book are cost-effective. Some, of course, do cost, but they should all bring a return on investment for you. Many of the strategies are FREE, just like the Core Elements.

Let's start with the second component of THE FORMULA: 'L' – Lead Generation...

Chapter Summary

To implement a strategy or Tactic in your business, it should be:

1. Proven
2. Universal
3. Quick
4. Easy to Implement
5. Long lasting
6. Cost Effective

CHAPTER 5:

LEAD GENERATION

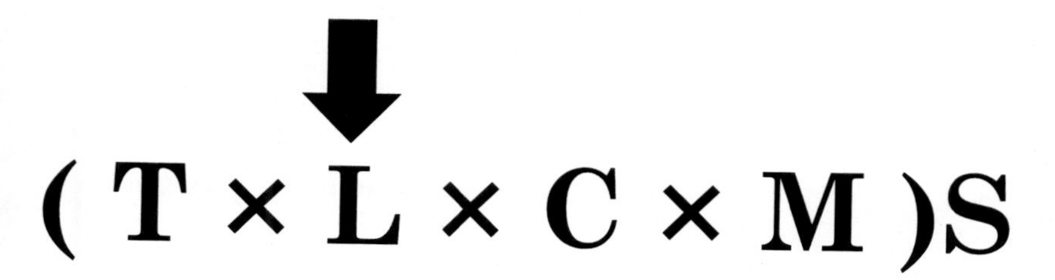

= EXPONENTIAL BUSINESS GROWTH

enerating leads or enquiries is, as I said earlier, the lifeblood of every business. Unfortunately, it is often also the costliest component of growing a business. Without a steady supply of leads or enquiries, you won't be able to acquire clients, customers or patients, so if you're actively looking to obtain more of them, then lead generation is a priority for you.

One big mistake I see most businesses make is that they use only one main method to generate leads. This is a dangerous and limiting approach. It's dangerous because if all you use is one tactic or strategy and for some reason it stops working, you've got a big problem on your hands. It's limiting because for THE FORMULA to be really effective it's important you use multiple lead-generation strategies. Then, of course, you get multiplied results.

What you need to do is take a slightly different approach to the lead-generation strategies you use. What I'm about to reveal is an approach that very few people outside our inner circle of coaching clients use. I promise it is the best way for you to determine which lead-generation strategies you should use for YOUR business. More importantly, it maximises your results, because you're not reliant on one tactic or strategy, or one main media. In this context, when I talk about 'media', I am referring to the way in which your lead-generation strategy is delivered to your target market.

Most people become reliant on one strategy and one media. In fact, more often than not, they simply use the same media and strategies that all their competitors are using.

This could mean two things:

- In most cases the best media isn't being used, and, as a result, neither are the best marketing tactics and strategies being used for the right target market(s).
- Existing marketing tactics and strategies are wasteful.

Furthermore, there can be a huge difference in results if you don't choose the correct media. It's been my experience that many businesses leave small fortunes on the table, simply because they have failed to **choose the correct media**.

The good news is that once you've defined the media, the lead-generation tactics and strategies select themselves.

This is a very simple yet highly effective way to determine the right media channels to use for your business.

First, let's look at the media channels available to you. As you can see, there are just three main media categories: **Published Media**, **E-Media** and **Direct Marketing Media**.

The table on the next page shows each media category and the associated strategies you can use for that particular media...

Media Category	Strategies
1. Published Media	• Classified Advertising • Newspaper, Magazine and Trade Press Advertising • Business Directory Advertising • Inserts • Radio Advertising • TV Advertising • Press Releases • Etc.
2. Direct Marketing Media	• Seminars • Letters • Postcards • Flyers • Joint Ventures • Newsletters • Leaflets • Telemarketing • Networking • Etc.

3. E-Media	• Website • Search Engines • Pay-Per-Click Search Engines • Facebook • LinkedIn • Twitter • Other Social Media • Press Releases • Etc.

So how do you choose the right media channel category and combination of media channels for your business?

First, and this is important:

I recommend you use all three media categories to reach your target market(s). Tests have proved that if you use a combination of all three categories, your results mushroom.

Second, to choose the right strategies, all you need to do is ask yourself the following two simple questions:

1. 'Where can my target market be reached?'
2. 'Where would the target market look to source our products or services?'

The answers to these two questions will help you to determine which marketing strategies to use. For example…

CHOOSING THE RIGHT STRATEGIES		
Where can the target market be found?	**Media Category**	**STRATEGIES**
At work (or in the business)	Direct Marketing Media	• Seminars • Letters • Postcards • Flyers • Joint Ventures • Newsletters • Leaflets • Telemarketing
At home	Direct Marketing Media	• Seminars • Sales Letter • Postcards • Flyers • Joint Ventures • Newsletters • Leaflets • Telemarketing
Subscribing To Trade Press	Published Media	• Classifieds • Trade Press • Inserts • Press Releases

Internet	E-Media	• Website • Search Engines • Pay-Per-Click Search Engines • Social Media • Press Releases
Local newspaper	Published Media	• Classifieds • Newspaper • Inserts • Press Releases

As you can see from the table above, you have numerous options in terms of the media category and then the strategies you should use. We'll get into the strategies shortly, but first I want to reinforce the one thing that will determine the success or failure of your lead generation: your irresistible offer.

The Importance of Your Irresistible Offer

We covered this earlier when I took you through the Core Elements. However, I want to get more specific at this stage.

I gave you numerous examples previously based on the types of offers that work really well. But when it comes to lead generation, it's hard to beat a **'lead magnet'**. These are based on the **'soft offers'** we spoke about earlier.

They're great because once created you can direct people to a specific page on your website, known as a **'landing page'** (more on this later) and deliver it FREE.

You would then use the other lead-generation strategies to promote the lead magnet (such as email, direct mail, etc.,) and then follow up with the people who requested the lead magnet (remember, only a small percentage of visitors will buy from you during their first visit, so follow-up is crucial to increase sales). Better still, this whole process is easy to automate, which I'll come on to in Chapter 8.

No matter what business you're in, you can use a lead magnet to attract your target market.

Your challenge then is to decide what your lead magnet is going to be. There are many different types of lead magnets. Here are my top six favourites...

The 6 Top Lead Magnets

#1: Special reports

These are best as PDFs (no cost to distribute). They should focus on giving your visitor (the target market) quality information they can't get anywhere else, information that demonstrates and reinforces your expertise and why they should ultimately choose you.

The key, as with many of the things you do, is to create a name for the report which is irresistible to your target market. For instance, here are examples that an accountant could use..

Seven Simple Yet Little-Known Accounting Tips That Add Thousands to Your Bottom-Line Profits

```
Twelve Legal Tax-Saving Loopholes That the Government
Doesn't Want You to Know About

The Seven Secrets to Creating a Mega-Profitable
Business
```

#2: Buyer guides

Buyer guides are highly desirable. Typically, they are written to explain the pitfalls of buying your product or service, and to explain the multitude of options available to the visitor. Obviously, the guide is skewed towards you and how you operate your business. For example:

```
Seven Common Pitfalls to Avoid When Choosing a
Commercial Printer for Your Small Business
```

#3: Training videos

Training videos have a high perceived value.

We have been offering training videos on our sites since September 2011, and they have transformed our results (which were already impressive).

Ideally, you should provide a transcript of each training video and a simple action plan or 'blueprint' to go with it.

Once again, your training videos should be focused on solving a big problem faced by your visitors. Think of it as the special report on video!

They do, of course, take time to create and produce, which is why so few people do them.

But they don't have to be expensive to create.

When we first started doing training videos, we did them in-house using a FREE and simple audio programme called Audacity, and Camtasia to record the training slides (created in PowerPoint). You can do the same.

#4: Seminars

We deliver a lot of free seminars. They are great because you interact personally with the audience and, of course, meet them in person.

The key, once again, is to deliver great content. Then, you're more than justified in delivering your sales pitch at the end of the seminar.

#5: Webinars

Online seminars, known now as 'webinars', can be very successful. There are now many great webinar platforms you can use to manage the whole process. We use WebinarJam, but the likes of GoTo Meeting and Zoom.us are excellent, too.

#6: Books

Your own self-authored book is a great giveaway. It represents fantastic value, whilst allowing you to demonstrate your expertise.

The key to using your book as a lead magnet is NOT charging for it; otherwise, you'll significantly reduce the number of people who request it.

It is, however, good practice to charge for postage and packaging, and this will also help to qualify people.

Examples of some of the lead magnets we use/have used

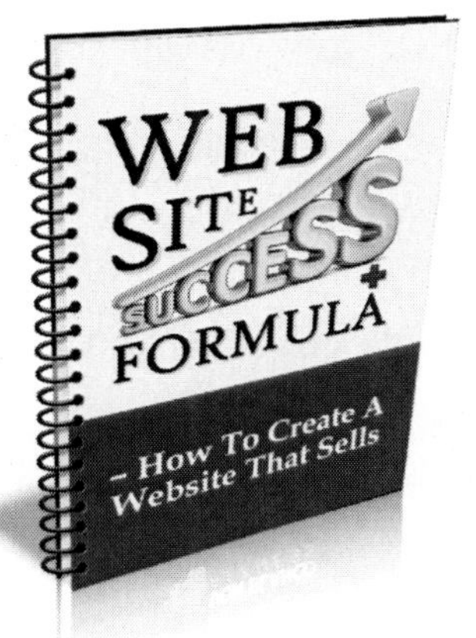

Our *Website Success Formula* special report

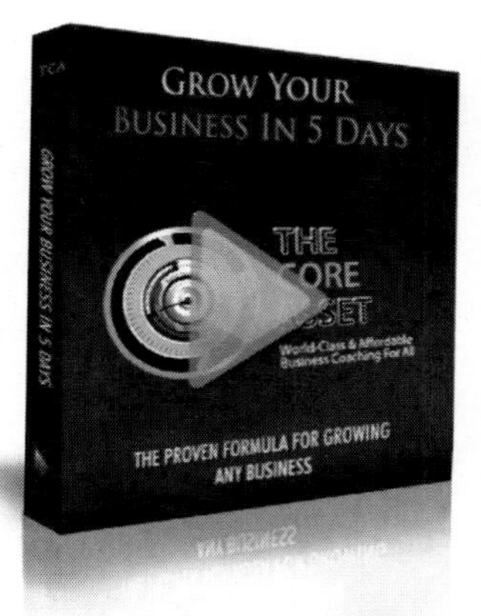

Our *Grow Your Business in 5 Days* video training course

The book we used to launch our sales and marketing network for accountants

DON'T MAKE THIS COMMON MISTAKE

It's very tempting when creating your lead magnet to think you need to hold back on content, hold back on your expertise, hold back on your insights and shortcuts.

THIS IS A BIG MISTAKE.

Give as much great content as you can.

Sure, some people will take what you've told them and implement it, but most won't.

Most want YOU to be the person to help them. But for them to think like this, you have to give value.

Over-deliver, and provide outstanding content.

I confess that in the early days of my first business, way back in 1995, I was fearful of this, but I learned that my results improved significantly as I gave more away.

No matter what you sell, you have so much expertise, so make sure you don't hold back when creating your free lead magnet.

Your results will soar when you take this approach.

So, for all your lead generation, you're going to use a powerful lead magnet to attract your target market. Agreed?

Now let me take you through my favourite lead-generation strategies. As I keep saying, no matter what business or industry you're in, these have UNIVERSAL application.

LEAD-GENERATION STRATEGY 1: Joint Ventures

The average business spends hundreds or thousands of pounds to generate leads or enquiries.

So how can you reduce the cost (in terms of time, as well as money) of acquiring prospects and customers? And what if you could do this with very little effort?

Joint Venture (JV) marketing is the method you use to capitalise on the trust and goodwill that exists between other non-competing companies and their clients, customers or patients.

How does it work?

It's quite simple really. Having set up a relationship with a Joint Venture Partner, they send a letter, email or similar (which you've prepared for them) to their customers, saying how great you are, and that if they ever need your type of product or service, they should give you a try.

Trust already exists between the JV partner and their customers, and the result is a very powerful form of referral or recommendation. Your products or services are being 'endorsed', and you'll be surprised at how many people become customers as a result.

This relationship is also known as a 'host-beneficiary alliance', in which the 'host' is the company with the customer base, and the 'beneficiary' is the business which gets custom from the host's customers.

Let's look at how you put together sales-generating joint ventures.

STEP 1: List the different types of products and services the customers buy before and after buying your product or service.

There are many circumstances in which people buy a complementary product or service, either before or after they've purchased another product or service.

For example, if you run a Microsoft Office training organisation, the customers would buy the latest version of the Microsoft Office software before they need your training services.

Going back one step further, they buy computer hardware before buying the software (or at least at the same time). This means you have two product categories you can focus on: software suppliers and hardware suppliers.

Another good example is an accountant. More often than not a potential client will see a bank manager before setting up their business. Therefore, the accountant could set up a JV with the bank in which the bank recommends the accountant's services to people starting a new business, as well as to those with established businesses.

Once you've decided on your different types of products and services, write them down.

STEP 2: Select the businesses that supply the products or services the customers buy before or after buying your product or service.

Now simply go online and search for the types of businesses that you've written down in Step 1.

You'll find dozens of businesses, small and large, who are potential JV partners for you. Simply write down the contact details of those that appeal to you most.

STEP 3: List the different types of businesses that have similar customers to you.

Now ask yourself this simple question: 'Which businesses serve the same type of customers as I do?'

Let me give you a couple of examples:

Wedding and Portrait Photographer: Their target market is people with joint incomes of over £100,000. They drive expensive cars, live in large houses, like to dress in designer clothes, eat at lavish restaurants, etc.

The types of businesses that have similar clients to them are high-end jewellery stores; car dealers selling BMW, Mercedes, Lexus, Jaguar, Aston Martin, Porsche, etc.; good-quality restaurants; private health clubs; up-market hair and beauty salons; designer wear retailers; etc.

Computer Training Organisation: They target the financial and legal sector, specifically the top 50 in each category (insurance, accountancy, legal, etc.). They've set up JV partnerships with graphic design companies, PR agencies, advertising agencies, etc.

In my coaching business, we partner with accountants, hotels and networking organisations, because they serve and have good relationships with people like you – owners of small or medium sized businesses.

No matter what product or service you sell, you'll be able to identify many different types of businesses who attract similar customers as you do. Write them all down.

STEP 4: Select the businesses that have similar customers to you.

Once again, go online and search for the types of businesses you identified in the previous step. Record their contact details.

STEP 5: Look at your own customers. Which ones sell products or services before or after you? Which ones have similar customers to you?

This is often overlooked by many people, but is the easiest and often most profitable strategy.

Your own clients, customers or patients are excellent people to set up JV partnerships with. They already trust you. And they already know how good your product or service is.

Go through your customer list, and select those who sell complementary products and services, and have similar customers to you.

STEP 6: Find out the name of the most senior person in each business you've selected.

You should now have your lists. Simply combine them together and start contacting each company to find out the name of the most senior person (you may have obtained this information previously for some of the businesses on your list).

It's very likely that your JV Partnership will have to be agreed by the 'top' man or woman, so it makes sense to get the name of this person in each company you've chosen.

Once you've done this, you've got your database of potential JV partners. Make sure you have (at least) the full address, postcode and telephone number of each company.

STEP 7: Decide on your endorsement offer.

Before you do anything else, you now need to decide on your endorsement offer. Ask yourself the following questions:

What incentive are you willing to give your endorsement partner?

This may differ with each relationship you set up, but it's important to know what you're prepared to 'give away'. Don't be stingy at this point. The more attractive you make the offer, the more likely you are to get good-quality JV partners.

For example, lawyers/solicitors will often pay estate agents a referral fee when the estate agent passes over their clients for conveyancing services.

This is often based on what the solicitor can give away whilst still making a profit on the sale/purchase.

The key is to work out what you can realistically afford to give away. In some circumstances, you may be willing to lose money on the initial transaction because the customer is worth much more to you in the long term (this takes into account lifetime customer value, as discussed earlier).

Alternatively, because all the companies on your list would be equally interested in YOUR customers, you can arrange a simple reciprocal endorsement (this is the easiest way to do it).

You endorse your partner to your customers, and they endorse you to their customers. Often this can be done by agreeing not to exchange any money, but to keep the additional business that comes to you both as a result of the relationship.

How are you going to administer the relationship?

One of the difficulties you may encounter when setting up your JV relationships is proving to the JV partner that you are trustworthy. If money is to change hands in return for successful customer acquisitions, the JV partner will want to make sure they are rewarded based on the terms of your agreement with them.

Here are several options:

1. Get the enquiry to go direct to your endorsement partner.

   If your partner takes all the enquiries and then forwards them on to you, they have a self-regulating process in place.

2. Get a simple letter of agreement drawn up.

   Make the relationship more formal by getting a simple document drawn up. When large sums of money are changing hands, it's advisable that you do this for both parties' sakes.

   It doesn't have to be a 15-page document; it just needs to cover the details of the relationship, what constitutes a 'payment', how and when the money will be paid, etc. We often use a simple two-page 'letter of agreement'.

3. The leads come direct to you, and you inform the JV partner when they come in.

   This does take trust from the JV partner, but you'll be surprised how often this can be done. Agree the frequency that you'll update the partner, and make sure you keep to the schedule.

What inducement are you going to offer your JV partner's customers?

This is very important. The reason why JV marketing works so well is that it's a win-win-win situation:

You win because you get more customers.

The JV partner wins on two counts. First, they gain financially or get more customers (reciprocal relationship), and second, they are offering their customers a product/service that will benefit them at a preferential rate, which promotes extra goodwill.

Finally, the customer benefits because you offer them an incentive they couldn't get if it were not for the relationship you have with the JV partner.

Therefore, the key to making the JV successful is to promote a special offer to your JV partner's customers. Even better, make it time-sensitive to get your response as soon as possible.

What can you offer?

Clearly there are a multitude of things you can offer. Remember, it has to be irresistible to your target market: a lead magnet! A lengthened free initial meeting/consultancy/analysis /discount on first order/free estimate, and then a discount on order, etc. Use your imagination and remember to have a deadline on the offer!

STEP 8: Write to each company with a JV partner recruitment sales letter.

Now you need to write to each company on your list. The objective of the letter is to get them to contact you. Use the Core Elements, but this time remember the target market is the JV partners themselves, not your clients, customers or patients.

Here are some important things you need to include in your letter in addition to the Core Elements.

You need to point out the following:

- Your product/service is non-competitive.
- It's not going to take away or supplement any income or profits their company would ordinarily have.
- It increases their profits.

- They don't have to do anything or spend a penny.
- You will create all the marketing material subject to their approval. You will pay for printing, postage and other costs. Say they can contribute if they wish to get a greater profit share.
- You'll indemnify them, and you'll unconditionally guarantee your products/services sold.
- The company can have all orders routed through them for verification if they wish.
- Tell them that it's pure profit for them on a continual basis.
- Educate them about the business and your product or service.

Here's an example of a successful letter to potential JV partners. It's from a flooring supply and fitting company.

**Increase Your Profits
Without Increasing Your Costs**

Dear <Name>,

If you could improve your profits through an added value service, without increasing your costs or losing focus, would you do it?

Well that's exactly what I can offer you. Using our unique introductory marketing and commission scheme, we would like to allow you to profit from recommending us to your prospects and clients.

Do you have the desire to add more value to your trusted customer relations and, in turn, grow extra streams of cash flow immediately? If the answer is yes, then our organisations can do business together!

Call me NOW on <Number> to arrange a no-obligation meeting that will explain in detail our service, and take you through our marketing plan and commissions agreement. Alternatively, if I haven't heard from you, I will call you in one week.

Thank you for your time.

Regards

<Name>

P.S. This is also a great opportunity for you to re-contact customers that haven't purchased from you in a while. This alone will generate some dormant sales for you, never mind the fact that they could also benefit from the added value service we offer!

STEP 9: Follow up each letter with a telephone call.

Even though your letter is written to generate a response from the potential endorsement partner, you'll improve your success rate if you do follow up.

STEP 10: Arrange meetings with interested parties.

Next, you need to arrange a meeting with the potential JV partner. You don't necessarily need to meet face-to-face; you can conduct this meeting over the telephone or via Skype/GoTo Meeting, etc.

Either way, this meeting is the chance to sell the JV idea. As long as the person has agreed to meet, there is an excellent chance they'll become a JV partner.

Try to get their decision at the meeting. If that isn't possible, make sure you keep following up.

STEP 11: Writing the endorsement letter/email

The endorsement letter is the letter YOU write for the JV partner to send out on their letterhead or via email to their customers, or the leaflet they hand out to their customers, etc. Of course, the JV partner's customers read the letter and assume it's come from them, not you.

This is very important. As I've said, JV marketing is all about other people endorsing (recommending) other products and services.

Once again, the endorsement letter is like a sales letter. However, one advantage you've got is that you don't need to build trust. Because it's coming from the JV partner, the trust already exists. In addition to the Core Elements, **here's what you need to include in your endorsement letter**:

- Highlight a specific problem your product or service solves.

- Mention the relationship the JV partner has with you and the benefit of that relationship.
- Discuss the special offer available if they reply quickly.
- Give them the response mechanism. For example, are they to telephone, go to a specific page on your website or email? And who do they contact: the JV partner or you?

Here's an example email we use from our accounting partners promoting our special report to their clients.

> Subject: The proven science behind growing your business
>
> Hi First Name,
>
> As a valued client, we are fully committed to helping you grow a better, more successful business.
>
> In fact, we've just discovered a scientifically proven way to grow your business and increase profits!
>
> It's taken over 20 years to prove …
>
> Undergone tens of thousands of tests …
>
> … and already more than 26,000 businesses have successfully applied it.
>
> It's called 'The Formula'.
>
> I believe it's the only proven scientific FORMULA for growing ANY small or medium sized business.

… and it's fascinating (and very simple).

If you haven't done so already, I urge you to take a look.

For a limited time, our friends at The Core Asset are giving FREE access to the 'Accelerate Formula Blueprint'. You can download your free copy here:

>> www.AccelerateFormula.co.uk

When prompted, please use the following 'Formula Unlock Code': XXXX

Discover the exact scientific FORMULA that thousands of small and medium sized businesses are using right now to increase their sales and profits.

Once again, THE FORMULA blueprint is currently FREE, and you can get it here, right now:

>> www.AccelerateFormula.co.uk

Kind regards,

JV partner's Name

P.S. Interestingly, there are only five elements to The Formula. Building your business is NOT rocket science, but it's been proven that it is a science.

STEP 12: Take action, and start your JV marketing campaign.

Okay. You've got the go-ahead, and you've found your first JV partner. Here's what you need to do next:

- Agree the endorsement letter/email/leaflet with the JV partner.
- Agree when the first mailing will be sent. Give yourself at least 2–3 weeks to prepare.
- Get the JV partner to start promoting.
- Get ready for replies. If you're getting the leads/sales direct to you, make sure you have a method for identifying how the person found out about you. This ensures you can distinguish between leads that are a direct result of the endorsement mailing and those that aren't.

How you should view the financial trade-off when using endorsement marketing.

- Let's say you currently spend £6,000 to bring in 100 customers, and that you gross £10,000 in sales from those 100 customers. The profit is £4,000.
- What if somebody were to give you 100 new customers, from whom you'd gross £10,000? These customers wouldn't cost a penny. Would you be willing to pay that person £5,000 for those customers? You should, because that person has saved you £6,000 in marketing expenses.
- You should always be prepared to pay the marketing costs if you are benefiting from the JV partner's customers.

(But if you can get away with not paying – all the better.) Often the promotion will be based around email, so the costs will be zero anyway!

- You can obviously negotiate on the revenue split. It may be 50–50, but it may make sense for you to give the initial profit to the JV partner, especially if you benefit from repeat purchases (lifetime customer value).

- The benefits to you and the JV partners are huge, no matter what the financial relationship is. You both generate money you would never have made. This income is brought in with little or no cost.

That's joint ventures. I've given you this level of detail because JVs are such a brilliant way to grow your business. They cost very little, and they can bring a rush of new customers, clients or patients into your company in no time at all!

Now let me take you through what is arguably the most important weapon in your armoury when it comes to lead generation: **your website**.

LEAD-GENERATION STRATEGY 2: Website

Obviously, you can use your website for generating leads, but it also applies to conversion and maximising value from customers. What you're about to discover now applies across the board, but I'll focus just on the lead-generation element for now.

First, let me say that, contrary to popular belief, your website should have only one primary objective:

The primary objective of your website is to generate leads and/or sales; it's not to 'showcase' your business (although it will); it's not to build your brand (although it will); and it's not to look good (although it will).

It should be in existence only to generate leads and/or sales.

This is very simple, but it's a point missed by 99% of small and medium sized businesses.

If all you do from this day forward is recognise this fact, I promise your website will become a true asset to you and your business.

I've been online since 1997. That was only four years after CERN gave us the World Wide Web.

I've made millions for my businesses and our clients' businesses online and continue to do so. I've sold products and services from £7 right up to £60,000 using the Internet, but none of it would have been possible without the overriding philosophy that a company website's only reason for being is to generate leads and/or sales.

Of course, I've made many, many mistakes and lost a fair amount of money online because of them, but I know what works. We help businesses in every imaginable sector create websites that fulfil their purpose (generating leads and/or sales), and the impact on the businesses sales and profits cannot be overstated.

Therefore, focusing on your website is critical if you want to make life easy for yourself (you can automate most things) and to quickly grow your business (which, of course, you do!)

Your website, when created correctly, should be seen as a central marketing hub that churns out leads or sales on a regular basis.

But since we're talking about lead generation, let me take you through the precise steps you need to take to ensure your website becomes a lead-generation 'machine'.

The good news is that it's not difficult, as long as you follow my advice. Even now, we conduct literally hundreds of tests (I'll show you some shortly), but we have a Framework that any business can use to achieve success.

In fact, I call it the ***Website Success Formula***. Here it is.

STEP 1: Set up landing pages with a clear objective.

When it comes to lead generation you need to realise that no matter how many pages your website has, each page should be set up as a 'landing page'. Also known as 'squeeze pages', they are created with one simple objective: to get the lead. That's it.

It's that simple.

Now you've got instant clarity.

You'll know what a lead is for your business. It could be

- a meeting (online or offline)
- a free estimate
- a quote
- an onsite visit
- a telephone call
- etc.

Often, however, you should use a FREE lead magnet, as discussed previously, in the step before the lead is generated.

Remember, **your lead magnet is your irresistible offer**.

The objective is still the same – to get the lead – but you use a lead magnet to get many more people into your funnel and therefore acquire more leads.

For example, let's say you're a commercial printer. The lead you're looking for may be a meeting with the business owner to discuss their print. But you create a lead magnet that's a free special report with the following title:

'How to Use Print to Build Your Brand and Double Your Sales Each Year'

... or something like that, but you get the picture.

The report details how to do this, and, of course, it's written to coincide with how you work and how your print achieves these kinds of results. The objective of your report is therefore to GET THE LEAD. So, at the end of the report you explain how these results can be achieved, and the first step is to meet with you.

Your call to action would then be to get the recipient to call the office or book a meeting using an online form.

Does that make sense?

You're using your lead magnet as a way to attract the target market, and then the lead magnet itself is used to convert that prospect into a lead.

Believe me, this is a tried-and-tested approach that works very, very well. Better still, because your objective is to get your prospect to request the lead magnet, your landing page is simply focused on this.

You don't need any 'bells' or 'whistles', or any Web design gimmicks.

STEP 2: Perfect page layout

So you've decided on your lead magnet; you now need to create the landing page itself.

We've carried out numerous tests on creating the perfect landing pages for every imaginable industry. There are several key elements that contribute to giving you the best possible results.

Headline

First, of course, you need a powerful headline at the top of the page. I'm repeating myself here because this is where most businesses make a huge mistake. Remember, the name of your business is NOT a powerful headline. By all means put your logo at the top, but make sure it doesn't overpower the headline.

Review the section in Chapter 3 on headlines; the same rules apply to your landing pages.

Hero shot

A 'hero shot' is simply an image on the page that supports the lead magnet. So, if you're using a free special report, put an image of the report on your page. This will immediately increase results.

Video

Video isn't compulsory, but it's definitely worth testing. It's rare that a page without video outperforms a page with video.

Your video doesn't have to be with you on screen. There are many, many viable alternatives.

When I first started out online back in 1996, video wasn't an option. Most people had only dial-up – can you remember how slow that was? But as broadband and now fibre optics have transformed download speeds, video has become a major asset to us all.

Video enables you to communicate in a very personal way with your visitors, and since most people take in more information from both visual and auditory presentations, video now plays an ever-increasing, important part in online success.

So, what's the purpose of your video?

That's simple:

It's to get the visitor to move to the next stage of your sales process and pick up your irresistible offer, whatever it is.

If that's a free special report, the video is created to ensure the visitor enters their details and downloads the report, and so on. If it's a webinar, the video explains why they should register, and so on. Are you starting to see the clarity this brings?

Incidentally, in terms of where to place your video, again this is simple: it should be positioned above the 'fold' so that when the page loads, the video can be seen immediately by the visitor without scrolling.

Creating the video

You have several options in terms of the types of video you can use:

- The business owner or spokesperson does it. It doesn't necessarily have to be the owner of the business or a member of staff – you can use actors – but it does show authority if you do it 'in person' (which, for professional services, is important). However, in many cases this is neither practical nor easy to do for many people. If that's the case, use one of the following options.
- PowerPoint–style video (which we also use often). Simply create a presentation along with a script, and use a screen video-capturing and audio programme to create the video. This is much easier than you may think. We use a great and inexpensive piece of software called Camtasia. You can get it here: www.camtasia.com
- Motion graphics and explainer videos also work well. You'll have seen these types of videos. They are basically cartoon-generated-type videos. You can do this yourself, but I recommend you use a professional company to do it for you. Search on Fiverr or Upwork, and you'll find

someone who specialises in this type of video. Expect to pay less than £250 for a five-minute video (easily long enough to persuade the visitor to get your irresistible offer).

The key with your video is not necessarily how you produce it. The most important thing is the script. If your script isn't persuasive, then the most beautiful, film-quality video won't work.

So spend your time crafting your message using the Core Elements, and then get the video produced around it.

The text must 'sell' the primary objective.

Any text you use on the page must also push or 'sell' your irresistible offer. Using the Core Elements on your pages with this level of clarity, your leads will multiply overnight.

Opt-in box

No matter what your irresistible offer is, you MUST get the contact details of your visitor. This is imperative, because it allows you to follow up (see below).

Tests have proved that getting just the email addresses of the visitors maximises the number of people who accept your offer, but there are justifiable reasons for asking for more information (make sure you're 'GDPR' compliant!).

Plus, whilst you should never ask for unnecessary information, again it's been proven that the more information you request, the higher the quality of lead.

It's a delicate balance. In an ideal world I'd want their full name, their email address, their full address and their mobile number. Then I could follow up with email, phone calls, SMS texts, and mail.

But unfortunately, it's not an ideal world!

As a minimum, we collect their first name and email address for lead magnets such as special reports. For our live seminars, we get all the information I described earlier. If I'm giving up my time, I want the room to be full of good prospects, not tyre-kickers, and I want to use a variety of marketing channels to get them to the seminar. If they don't buy at the seminar, I want to be able to contact them in several different ways.

You just need to give this some thought.

Don't ever ask for information that you're never going to use. For example, if you ask for their mobile phone number and you're not actually going to text them or call them, what's the point?

Your opt-in box should also be placed above the fold. So, if you're using video, place the video on the left of the page, and the opt-in box on the right.

STEP 3: Automated follow-up

To maximise the value of each visitor and to put your lead generation on autopilot (more on this in Chapter 8), you need to create an automated, step-by-step follow-up system for the visitors who request your irresistible offer.

Your opt-in box is used to collect the relevant information from the visitor. It's then HOW you use this information that's important, and when you use it correctly (as I'm about to outline), your leads, and therefore your sales, will go through the roof.

For effective follow-up, you need a fully automated system, one that runs on autopilot every minute, every hour, every day of every year.

Your follow-up will be carried out depending on the information you requested in your opt-in box.

Obviously, if all you asked for was their email address, you're going to be using only email to follow up. If you also asked for their mobile number, you can add SMS texts, phone calls, etc.

There are a multitude of great providers that automate this whole follow-up sequence for you.

We use Infusionsoft and have done pretty much since it was formed. My staff used to call it 'Confusionsoft'!

But it is much simpler now than it used to be, and we love it. It automates our entire business, not just the sales and marketing side of things.

If email follow-up is all you need, then I would recommend AWeber. AWeber has been around right from the beginning of the Web, and it's an amazing email 'autoresponder'. It has the industry's highest email delivery rates, and their system is very easy to use.

It's FREE for the first month, and then it depends on the volume of subscribers or opt-ins on your list. Prices start from around $20 for 500 subscribers and unlimited emails.

You can sign up for a free account here:

http://coreasset.aweber.com

Next, and critically, you need to decide on the frequency of your emails/texts, etc.

For now, let's focus on sending emails.

The first email should, of course, be delivered to the subscriber (the visitor that entered their name and email address on your website to receive your irresistible offer) immediately, thanking them for requesting your offer. If relevant, it should also include the link to the lead magnet, if it's a report or video course, etc.

Here's a simple example:

Subject: [THANK YOU] The Accelerate Formula (download instructions)

Hi ~Contact.FirstName~

Thank you for requesting The Accelerate Formula Blueprint. If for whatever reason you weren't redirected to the download page, you can download THE FORMULA from here.

I've also prepared a video for you, explaining how to get the Formula working immediately in your business! It also includes two additional elements that almost always multiply the results of THE FORMULA by a factor of 4 (yes f-o-u-r).

This is the exact same Formula that thousands of small and medium sized businesses are using to achieve startling increases in their sales and profits.

```
If you haven't already done so, you can
access the video here.

Thanks again ~Contact.FirstName~.

Enjoy!

To your success,

- Steve

P.S. Once you apply The Accelerate Formula
then add our step-by-step scientific
approach, you'll have everything you'll ever
need to create the micro-business you always
wanted. It's not rocket science, but it is a
science. Find out exactly how to do it here:

>> Accelerate Formula + Science VIDEO
```

I'm going to let you into a secret here that will probably astonish you. We've tested frequency to the *n*th degree. For most businesses, **sending an email EVERY day** will work best for you, but you don't ever want to be emailing less than once every seven days! We email our subscribers every day.

Yes, this takes effort, but probably no more than 30 minutes a day.

You may be shocked at that and feel it's too frequent, but anything less and your results tail off alarmingly.

Of course, you now have to write your series of emails.

As you can imagine, there's an art to writing effective emails. I've been doing it since 1996, and it took me several years before I really found out how to do it right. My technique is unusual, but if you've opted-in to any of our other courses or videos, you'll see what I mean.

The key is to weave a story into every email you write. It should end with a link to you and your offer, but the story makes the email interesting, and makes it hard for the recipient to stop reading.

Here's an example. It's one I wrote for a client. He runs the leading commercial property sales business in Germany. This is one of the emails subscribers receive after requesting one of his special reports. This particular special report is called 'What's My Commercial Property Really Worth?'

> Subject: [Commercial Property] A true and tragic story …
>
> Hi Firstname,
>
> I mentioned yesterday that 95% of valuations are WRONG.
>
> In fact, I trust only ONE 'valuation expert' locally … and even he now reverts to me when people come to him to sell their commercial property.
>
> Here's why …
>
> A few years ago, my valuation buddy said this one particular commercial property was worth €625,000.
>
> I said €450,000 max.
>
> I got a buyer for €450,000.

There were three owners of this property.

Two said 'yes let's go with Roberto's value and buyer'.

One said 'No'.

No sale.

18 months later it was sold for €300,000.

Ouch!

FACT … even good valuers start normally 30% overpriced, and this *will result in losses of 30%, 40%, even 50%*.

Why take the risk?

For example, in the last 13 years alone (except for three justified exceptions) I sold all my clients' commercial properties within the agreed purchase price range and all within 12 months (the industry norm is 2.5 years!).

That's because of many factors, but primarily because the valuation in each case was RIGHT.

Let me ensure you get the maximum price for your commercial property and sell it in the minimum time.

To get things moving, call me at <**Number**>, or if you have any questions, simply reply to this email. Thank you.

Kind regards,

Robert

P.S. Selling your commercial property in the quickest time possible, for the maximum value has EVERYTHING to do with **getting the valuation right from Day 1.** Let the experts take care of it for you. Why take the risk? Even if you have a valuation report, it's got a 99% chance of being wrong (see special report on why)!

To ensure you sell your commercial property for the highest price in the minimum time, call me at <**Number**>, or, if you have any questions, simply reply to this email. Thank you.

You've now got a landing page that 'sells' and a follow-up system that will convert more visitors into good-quality leads. But there's one final piece of the jigsaw missing: the traffic itself, or, more importantly, targeted traffic.

STEP 4: Targeted Traffic

There's no point in having a great landing page if the right people don't visit it. READ THAT AGAIN!

Remember, we've created a landing page that's set up to convert the visitor into a LEAD. And here's the thing:

Once you know it's working well, you should see that page as a central 'marketing hub', a hub to which you send all your traffic. The reason why most marketing doesn't work is that business owners are using strategies that send people to their website, which has a terrible conversion. But think about it ...

Once you've got a landing page that converts (as you will), it makes complete sense to send as many people to it as you can. Agreed?

Here's what it looks like:

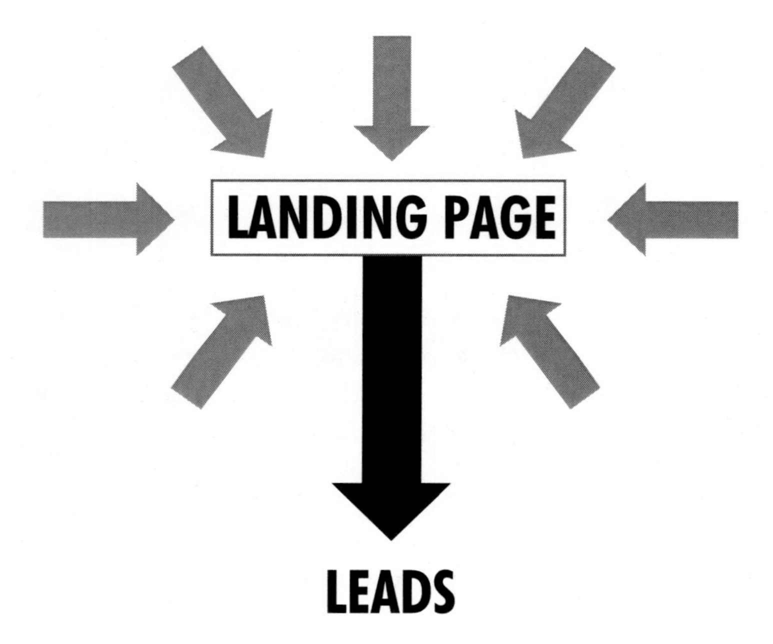

The arrows pointing to the landing page represent the traffic sources from your marketing tactics and strategies, and the big black arrow represents your funnel (which includes your follow-up sequence), which churns out a constant supply of leads for your business.

That's the model you're setting up when you follow my advice, and I can assure you, it will transform your entire lead generation.

Better still, you now have a 'system' working 24/7 for you, and you know that whatever lead-generation tactics and strategies you use to generate visitors/traffic to the landing page, they're going to be successful.

You use the Core Elements in all your lead-generation tactics and strategies, which means they'll be effective, and then they go to a landing page that's effective. The result is simple: you get many more leads that you can convert into sales.

But before we move on, there are a few more important things you need to be aware of when it comes to optimising the results of your landing pages.

Optimise your conversion rate before worrying too much about traffic.

There's no point in having a great landing page if no one visits it. Likewise, there's no point in getting thousands of visitors to your website if it doesn't yield results. The website success formula will help you get great results from your landing pages, but most elements can be improved, in time, with TESTING.

What you're looking to transform is your CONVERSION RATE.

Conversion rate (expressed as a percentage) in this context is a measure of the number of leads or opt-ins your landing page generates divided by the number of UNIQUE visitors (see below) during a set period of time. Obviously, the higher the percentage, the better!

You can go mad on testing, and you can test absolutely everything on the page, but in my experience the elements to test that will give you the biggest potential boost in results are as follows:

- headline
- hero shot
- video
- opt-in box

For example, here's a screenshot showing a test we ran on simply changing the headline on the same landing page.

Variation B	41.8%	BASELINE	66	158	50 %
Variation C	34.5%	-7.3%	38	110	50 %

Notice the average conversion of the two pages is 40.5%. This is the type of result you can achieve when you use the Core Elements and the landing page approach I've just taken you through.

The two headlines we tested against each other were …

THE FORMULA – The Secret to Quickly Building a Successful Small Or Medium Sized Business and ...

THE FORMULA - The Breakthrough System to Quickly Multiply the Sales and Profits of Your Small Or Medium Sized Business

Which one do you think won?

Now you might think a 7.3% difference isn't amazing (I'm delighted with it, because over months and years this will make a big difference to our results). But remember, this is the difference between two already highly optimised landing pages, each with what I would call a world-class headline. Just think of the difference there will be between your existing headline (which is likely to be the name of your business) compared to a world-class headline. You're talking hundreds of percent!

... and that's just the headline!

(By the way, the top headline worked best!)

LEAD-GENERATION STRATEGY 3: Google Ads

Since Google created AdWords (now 'Google Ads') in October 2000, it has helped us and countless others to generate millions in sales. At one point (in the early days admittedly) we were spending over £15,000 a month on AdWords for just one business, but it was giving us a return on investment (ROI) of over 1,500%.

We still run a Google Ads campaign for our businesses today, of course, and it currently yields a very healthy ROI of 900% – yes, nine times the return (every £2,000 we spend generates around £18,000 in membership income).

That's one heck of a marketing strategy!

But like everything, there are many mistakes that can be made when it comes to Google Ads. And yes, we've probably made all of them.

There are other PPC (pay-per-click) search engines to consider (such as Bing – Microsoft's PPC model), but Google will give you the best return if you follow my advice.

I've included it in this book because it's such an amazing lead-generation strategy that every business on the planet can use.

There are many complexities with Google Ads, but I'm going to take you through the fundamentals and principles which Google will never change. As long as you adhere to these, I promise Ads will be a very lucrative strategy for you.

Google's business objective

Google's overriding business objective is to continue to give its users (people searching) an amazing experience. In other words, no matter what search term a user enters, Google will endeavour to return aligned results for that search. If you think about it, that's why we all use Google, and that's why they are, by far, the world's number-one search engine.

So even though their billions are generated through advertising revenue on Google and YouTube, it's focus is and always will be on its users. Google knows that as long as they keep providing a world-class search experience, people will continue to use it, and that the ad revenue will then take care of itself.

Therefore, Google has developed its initial AdWords programme to ensure this objective is met.

It wasn't always like this. When they first started out, their pay-per-click ad model was the same as everyone else's. It was a free-for-all, like the Wild West. Advertisers were using ads that weren't necessarily linked to the search term, and Google was in danger of not delivering on its promise to users.

So they completely changed their model, and they are now extremely strict about who advertises and what keywords their ads are aligned to, and anyone that goes against this overriding philosophy is banned.

I think it's genius.

Everyone wins: the users, the advertisers and Google.

The good news is that you have only to play by Google's rules, and your campaign will be successful.

No matter what changes Google makes in the future, you can be certain that their ultimate goal of making sure they provide a world-class search experience for their users will never change.

I'm not going to go into massive detail about setting up your Ads campaign (that's another book in itself and Google have a great help centre with videos and supplementary details), but I *am* going to give you the primary basics that will ensure your campaign is successful right out of the gate.

What exactly is Google Ads?

Just for clarity, Google Ads are the small adverts that appear at the top and bottom of Google after you've performed a search and the results appear.

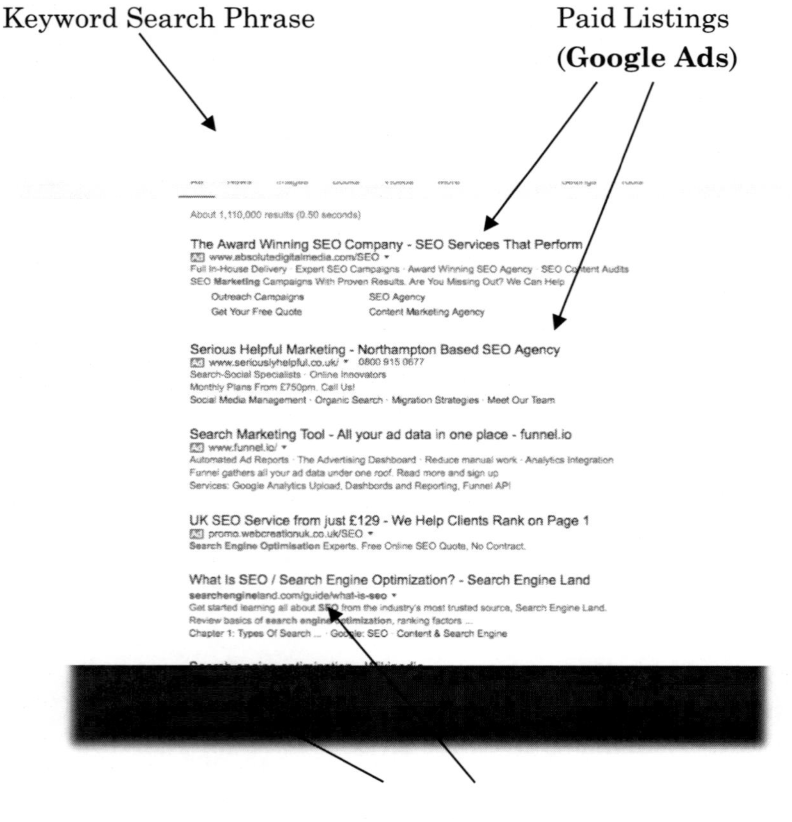

are optimised and ranked higher by Google – <u>not</u> paid advertising)

STEP 1: Know the basics

How long does it take to set up a campaign?

It takes just a few minutes to set up a campaign (but I recommend you follow my advice here to ensure you set it up properly). Within 15 minutes of setting up a campaign, you can start getting highly targeted visitors onto your website/landing page.

It is quite simply one of the most instant and immediately effective advertising media in the world.

How do you pay for Ads?

You pay only when people click on your adverts. This is unlike virtually every other type of advertising, for which you usually pay in advance, regardless of whether anyone responds or not!

How much does it cost each time someone clicks on my ad (cost per click)?

There are a number of factors involved in determining how much you pay every time someone clicks on your ad. Unfortunately, Google keeps the exact calculations close to their chest. What we do know is the following:

- The position of your ad will determine how much you pay. For example, all things being equal, if your ad is placed at position 1, then you will pay more than if your ad was placed at position 2, and so on. However, see below.
- Google rewards ads that have a high 'click-through rate' (the percentage of people who click on your ad from the number of impressions [how many times your ad was

shown]). So, if your ad has a much better click-through rate compared to other advertisers that you're competing with, then your ad would cost less, even if it's above other advertisers! Yes, that's right – Google rewards better ads by reducing your cost per click.

- You can set the maximum cost per click. That means you can minimise your cost exposure when you combine it with the maximum spend per month.
- You could pay anything from, say, 10p/cents to well over £/$10 per click for highly competitive keywords. That's why your keyword analysis is so important!

How do I choose the right keywords?

I go into much more detail about this later, but for now your keywords should be the keywords that your target market would use to find you or your type of product or service.

STEP 2: Create your keyword list, keyword groups and negative keyword list.

Before creating your account in Google Ads, I recommend you first carry out the following:

- KEYWORD RESEARCH: Since Google Ads works on keywords and keyword phrases, the work you do to identify your keywords is essential to your success. DO NOT RUSH THIS.

  I recommend you invest in Word Tracker (www.wordtracker.com). At the time of writing, it costs less than $30 a month, and you can cancel your subscription at any time. Join for one month, and during this time you should have completed all your research so you can cancel your account. The help tutorials are excellent, and it's a very straightforward programme to use to identify your best keywords.

Google have their own, free keyword tool, which is also excellent. It's called 'Keyword Planner'. They keep moving it around, but once you login to your account you'll find it under 'Planning'.

Once you've carried out your research, you'll have a long list of keywords. For example, here's a section of the list of keywords (the first 30 in alphabetical order) I created from our keyword research, looking to target accountants who are looking to grow their firms...

Keywords	Global Monthly Searches	Local Monthly Searches
accountancy marketing	1300	320
accountancy practice management	880	260
accountancy telemarketing	36	36
accountant advertisement	1900	390
accountant advertising	3600	720
accountant marketing	3600	720
accountant website	14800	1600
accountant websites	5400	720
accountants website	6600	1300
accountants websites	2400	590
accounting advertising	6600	880
accounting advertising ideas	46	0
accounting and marketing	12100	1300
accounting firm advertising	390	22

accounting firm marketing	1000	73
accounting firm marketing plan	140	0
accounting firm sales	720	16
accounting for advertising	6600	880
accounting in marketing	12100	1300
accounting marketing	12100	1300
accounting marketing letters	91	28
accounting marketing strategies	320	16
accounting practice management	4400	720
accounting sales	33100	2400
accounting services marketing	590	36
accounting slogans	720	73
accounting website	22200	1900
accounting websites	6600	880
advertising accounting	6600	880

This is great, but you're not finished yet.

- KEYWORD GROUPS: What you now need to do is take your entire keyword list and create 'keyword groups'.

  This is very important.

  Why?

  Because you need to closely match your ads to your keywords (the more focused your keywords and ads are, the better your results), and you can't do that if you have a long and diverse list of keywords. But don't worry; this will all make sense as I take you through the example.

  This approach stems back to Google's objectives of making sure every search produces great results for the user. The more defined your keyword groups are, and the more aligned to the search term, the better your results will be.

  What you want to do, therefore, is create groups into which your keywords can be sorted.

  Let's take my example above for the first 30 keywords. Notice that although they are all related to marketing for accountants, they differ considerably. So what we want to do is cluster similar keywords together and create a group for them.

  So here's what I did:

Group	Group Name	Keywords
1	Accountancy Marketing	accountancy marketing
2	Accountant Marketing	accountant marketing
3	Accounting Firm Marketing	accounting firm marketing
4	Accounting Sales	accounting firm sales
		accounting sales
5	Accounting Website	accountant website
		accountant websites
		accountants website
		accountants websites
		accounting website
		accounting websites
6	Accounting And Marketing	accounting and marketing
		accounting firm marketing plan
		accounting in marketing
		accounting marketing
		accounting marketing letters
		accounting marketing strategies
		accounting services marketing
		accounting slogans

7	Accounting Advertising	accountant advertisement
		accountant advertising
		accounting advertising
		accounting advertising ideas
		accounting firm advertising
		accounting for advertising
		advertising accounting
8	Accounting Practice Management	accountancy practice management
		accounting practice management
9	Accountancy Telemarketing	accountancy telemarketing

As you can see, I've created nine keyword groups and then attached each keyword to one of those groups. Now we have nine groups of tightly matched keyword groups for which we can create highly targeted ads.

Now you're ready for the next step, which is also crucial to your success.

- NEGATIVE KEYWORDS: This is a great feature that Google provides. Here's how Google explains about negative keywords.

> Choosing negative keywords for your campaign is like writing the guest list for your birthday party. Some keywords might create unwanted impressions and clicks, or, in the case of party guests, unpleasant moments that you'd prefer to avoid. Good thing you can add negative keywords to your campaign – or cross certain people off your guest list.
>
> Negative keywords can help you reach the most interested customers, reduce your costs, and increase your return on investment. You can add your own negative keywords, or get ideas from us.

So your negative keyword list is AS IMPORTANT as your keyword list.

It reduces unwanted clicks, therefore increasing your results whilst simultaneously reducing your costs.

So how do you create your negative keyword list? There are many ways to do it, but here's what I advise.

- Take the main keyword group name and insert it into Word Tracker or Google's Keyword Planner, or you can use the following free tool (you get 30 free searches):

  http://www.wordstream.com/negative-keywords

- Now look at all the keywords it throws up and remove a word or phrase that shows up that is NOT related to your product/service. For example, I entered the keyword group 'Accounting and Marketing' into the WordStream tool, and it suggested the following words (the ones in **bold**) that could be negative keywords for us.

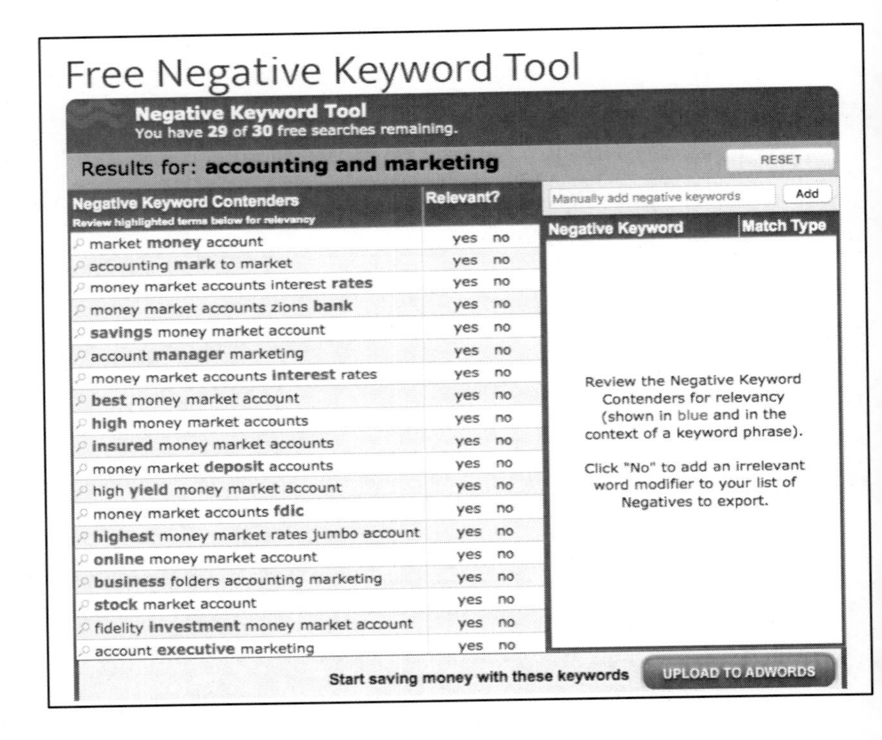

Simply go through all the keywords and select the words that you know are not relevant to your chosen keywords. THE LONGER THE LIST, THE BETTER.

So, for example, I would add the following negative keywords from the list above:

- ✓ money
- ✓ mark
- ✓ rates
- ✓ bank
- ✓ savings
- ✓ manager
- ✓ interest
- ✓ high
- ✓ insured
- ✓ deposit
- ✓ yield
- ✓ fdic
- ✓ highest
- ✓ stock
- ✓ investment
- ✓ executive

I would NOT enter the following in my negative keyword list, because there is a chance these words would be okay when associated with our keywords:

- X best
- X online
- X business

This is really easy to do (although few people do it), and hopefully you can see that it will make a massive difference to the success of your campaign.

STEP 3: Activating your Google Ads account

- Type 'Google Ads' into the Google search box. The first ad at the top of the page will give you your local Ads sign-up URL.
- At the time of writing, you can phone Google direct and they will help set up the campaign for you. I recommend you do this. They are very helpful, and they will guide you through the process.
- Whether you get Google to do it or you do it yourself, you're ready to set up your account in Google Ads. This is easy. Just follow the instructions. There are, however, a few things you need to be clear on ...
- Campaign name: This is really just about good administration/housekeeping. I prefer to create a campaign for each closely aligned set of keyword groups. So, in the example above, all nine keyword groups would be in a campaign we could call 'Accountants Marketing'. If we targeted, say, lawyers or solicitors, we would create another campaign titled 'Lawyer Marketing'.
- Campaign type: You have the following options:
    1. **Search network only:** The campaign displays your ads on Google search only (i.e. the Google

website) and their search partners (other search engines).

2. **Display network only:** The campaign displays your ads only on Google's partner websites (you can choose which websites your ads appear on).
3. **Search and Display Networks:** The campaign displays your ads on both the search and display networks.
4. **Video:** Don't select video yet – you need to master Ads first.
5. My advice is to initially choose option 1.

- Locations: This is where you can define where in your country – or, in fact, where in the world – you want your ads to appear. Look back at your target market for the geographic location(s) you are targeting customers from.

  Google allows you to choose entire countries, cities or even towns. If you click on the 'Advanced' tab, you can even select a radius (number of miles around a set location). This is geographic targeting of the highest order. Use it.

- Bidding and Budget: You can change this once you've entered the details in the setup section. So, for now, just enter £/$2 in the 'Default Bid' and £/$20 per day in the 'Budget'.

- Ad Group Name: You've already created your ad group names, so enter the first ad group name (you can set up your other ad groups once your campaign is set up).

- Create an Ad: This is the most important part. Remember, without a decent ad, the number of visitors you'll get will reduce, and you'll end up paying Google more, because your click-through rates will be low. Google really make it worthwhile to create good ads, so spending time here is very important.

  Google place tight restrictions on what you can and can't do, as well as on how much space (characters) they allow for your ads.

  Use the following guide on creating great ads:

  1. Headline 1 and 2 (25 characters): You must test this, of course, but we have found that using the keyword in one of the two headlines increases click-throughs most of the time.

  2. Description Line 1 and Line 2 (35 characters each): Now you use your description to promote your offer. It's this description that will determine if you get the click or one of your competitors does instead.

     Type your keyword into Google search and review competitor ads. What do they say? How can you entice people even more to click on your ad?

     Don't agonise too much over your ads. Yes, you should take time to craft persuasive ads, but because Google has such great testing architecture, you can improve your ads quickly. It's best to launch and then keep improving.

THAT BEING SAID, I ADVISE YOU TO CREATE AT LEAST TWO ADS FOR EACH KEYWORD GROUP.

When you create your ad, Google shows you what the ad will look like.

3. Display URL: This is the Web address you want displaying in your ad. It has to resemble the destination URL, otherwise Google will reject your ad. For example, if your keyword is 'accountant marketing' and your destination URL is 'www.abc.com/landing-page-1', your display URL must be something like

   'www.abc.com/accountant/marketing';

   it can't be something like

   'www.xyz.com/accountant/marketing'.

   Incidentally, Google gives you 15 characters each for the two words after your main URL (in this case I've used 'accountant' and 'marketing'). Tests have proved that the closer you can match these two words to each keyword, the better.

4. Destination URL: This is the EXACT Web address that you want the visitor to land on when they click your ad. In my example above that would be: 'www.abc.com/landing-page-1'

5. Keywords: Simply cut and paste your researched and shortlisted keywords into the box for the

relevant keyword group. You can enter your negative keywords later.

IMPORTANT NOTE ABOUT KEYWORD MATCHING OPTIONS

At this point it's worth informing you that there are four types of keyword matching options available to you. I urge you to read Google's explanation of this, but I've cut and pasted their introduction here.

> *In general, the broader the keyword matching option, the more traffic potential that keyword has; while the narrower the keyword matching option, the more relevant that keyword will be to someone's search. Understanding these differences can steer you in choosing the right keyword matching options and can help you improve your return on investment (ROI).*
>
> *To use a particular keyword match type, you can use special punctuation. Each keyword match type triggers ads to show in different ways. The chart below serves as an introduction to the different matching options, and we'll give more information on each option in the sections below (see next page) ...*

Use this match type ...	with this punctuation ...	to trigger your ad on.	Example
broad match	none	synonyms, related searches and other relevant variations	*adopt kittens chicago*
broad match modifier	+keyword	close variations but not synonyms or related searches	*+adopt +kittens +chicago*
phrase match	'keyword'	a phrase and close variants of that phrase	*'adopt kittens' chicago*
exact match	[keyword]	an exact term and close variants of that exact term	*[adopt kittens chicago]*
negative match	-keyword	searches without the term	-puppies

I advise you to use all options EXCEPT 'broad' to begin with (plus, of course, your negative keywords), and then review your campaign at regular intervals to remove keywords that aren't working.

STEP 4: Adding your other keyword groups to the campaign

Once you've completed the setup, you need to add your negative keywords and your other ads to the campaign. Remember, Google will 'split-test' all your ads. This means Google will rotate your ads equally every time there is a search for one of your keywords. They then provide the data for each ad, which will show you which ads are performing best.

Once you've finished setting up the campaign, you then need to add your other keyword groups to the campaign.

STEP 5: Creating your landing pages

The good news is that as long as you follow my earlier advice on creating powerful landing pages, your campaign will be successful.

You use the same rules for your Google Ads landing pages; however, we want to show Google and the user that when they click on your ad, the page they go to is highly relevant for the keyword entered.

So what you do is weave your keyword into the landing page.

For example, include it in your headline; include it in the text on the page; include it on your opt-in box, etc. Don't over-use it, though; add it only where it makes sense.

Now you've got a landing page designed to get results, and enhanced, because it's highly relevant to every keyword or keyword group you're using in your campaign.

That means Google will reward you by reducing your cost per click, and visitors will reward you by taking action.

Please note: DO NOT miss this step out. You now have the necessary tools to create response-generating landing pages. By making each landing page relevant to every keyword or ad group, you multiply your results. Yes, it takes more time to do this than simply sending visitors to your website or one landing page that gets all the visitors (which is how many people do it!), but it's worth it. Invest the time to create your Google Ads campaign properly, and your results will astonish you.

STEP 6: Testing your ads

As I mentioned above, you've created multiple ads so you can test and improve your campaign. In the first few weeks and months you will want to monitor and manage your campaign every day. The changes you make can be significant.

Pause (don't delete) ads that underperform, and create another ad to test. Keep testing your ads until you exhaust your options and you get to a point where your best-performing ad can't be beaten.

STEP #7: Managing your keywords and keyword groups

In addition to testing and managing your ads, you need to focus on your keywords, keyword groups and negative keywords.

Google have some great reporting tools for this. Their best report is the 'Keyword Details' report. This report shows you the actual real-life searches people made for every click on your ads. It's a great insight into your campaign.

Here's how to use it:

1. Create separate keyword groups for high-click-through keywords: The keyword searches that are relevant and get the most traffic should be stripped out of their current keyword group and have their own separate keyword group.

   For example, look at the partial list of one of our

Filter Columns

Back to Keywords

Learn how customers are finding your ad! Here, you'll see the actual searches that triggered your ad and led to a click. These terms were matched to your ads based on the ke

To make sure you can see data in this report, choose a date range that includes clicks on your keywords.

Download

Search term	Match type	Added/Excluded	Clicks	Impr.	CTR	Avg. CPC	Cost	Avg. Pos.
			752	53,569	1.40%	£2.13	£1,601.19	3
marketing for accountants	Exact match	Added	126	1,573	8.01%	£2.00	£251.83	1.6
telemarketing for accountants uk	Broad match	None	7	39	17.95%	£2.57	£17.99	2.6
marketing ideas for accountants	Exact match	Added	7	58	12.07%	£1.85	£12.98	1.5
accountancy marketing strategy	Broad match	None	6	19	31.58%	£2.28	£13.69	1.8
internet marketing for accountants	Phrase match	None	6	29	20.69%	£1.76	£10.53	1.4
accountant marketing ideas	Broad match	None	5	6	83.33%	£1.52	£7.59	1.3
marketing for accountants uk	Exact match	Added	5	30	16.67%	£1.45	£7.24	1.9
marketing tips for accountants	Exact match	Added	5	18	27.78%	£1.08	£5.38	1
internet marketing bible for accountants the complete guide to using social media and online advertising including facebook twit	Broad match	None	4	273	1.47%	£0.95	£3.79	1.1
marketing accountancy firms	Broad match	None	4	4	100.00%	£1.91	£7.63	1.2
accountancy marketing services	Broad match	None	4	5	80.00%	£2.72	£10.89	1.6
marketing for accounting practices	Exact match	Added	4	6	66.67%	£1.20	£4.81	1.2
best marketing tools for accountancy practices	Broad match	None	3	3	100.00%	£1.88	£5.65	1.3

For the keyword phrases showing, it would be prudent to create separate keyword groups for the top eight keywords.

2. Add negative keywords: Look through the list and check to make sure all the searches are relevant. If not, add to your negative keyword list.

   You'll notice from the example above that all the search terms shown are relevant. This is because after continual monitoring and improving, it's rare that a search will occur that isn't relevant. However, further down the list was the following search term:

   `find advertisement for graduate accountant`

   That's clearly not relevant to us, so 'graduate' was added to our negative keyword list. That click cost us £3.26, so imagine allowing your campaign to run and run without pruning and managing it in this way.

   You could end up paying significantly more than you need to and get the same results. Spending the least amount possible to get the highest return possible is what you should focus on.

   And that's how you set up a successful Google Ads campaign. There is more to it, but these elements will never change, because of Google's business objectives and their commitment to making their search the best on the planet.

***

Now let's move onto the third part of THE FORMULA: 'C' – Conversion...

Chapter Summary

- Choose the correct media to suit your target audience. Use all three types – Published, Direct Marketing and Electronic media.

- Lead Magnet – Soft Offers

  Top 6 Lead Magnets:

  1. Special reports
  2. Buyers guides
  3. Training videos
  4. Seminars
  5. Webinars
  6. Books

- **Lead Generation**

  Strategy 1: Joint Ventures

  Strategy 2: Website

  Strategy 3: Google Ads

CHAPTER 6:

CONVERSION

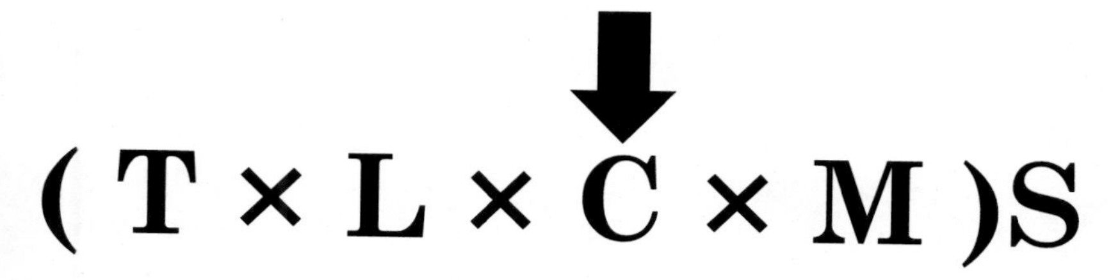

= EXPONENTIAL BUSINESS GROWTH

any business owners spend a considerable amount of time, effort and money generating leads. However, there's no point in generating a ton of leads if you convert only a small percentage of them into clients, customers or patients. Agreed?

Even if the business sells a high-priced product or service, and one or two customers from a total of 100 or more leads is profitable, just think what the business would achieve if it converted 5 or 10 or 15 times that number?

Concentrating more on 'converting' leads into clients, customers or patients will ensure two things:

1. You'll transform the business overnight.
2. You'll maximise the investment you make on ALL your lead-generation strategies.

The good news is that putting a 'system' in place to convert more leads into clients, customers or patients is simple and costs very little (if anything at all).

Conversion is therefore one of the key leverage points in your business and one where you can make quick and instant gains.

One of the areas in business where I have become highly competent is in the formation of systems. Long before I read Michael Gerber's brilliant *E-Myth*, I was creating internal and external systems to make sure as many of the things we did happened in an orderly and predictable fashion, enabling many efficiencies and desired outcomes to be enjoyed.

One of the areas where systems play a big part, but an area where few businesses apply them, is conversion and creating what I call a *sales conversion system*.

So what is a sales conversion system?

In simple terms, a sales conversion system is a set of logical steps from the moment a lead is generated to the moment the sale is made, with the sole goal being to generate as many sales as possible.

Remember, the lead or enquiry could be from a prospect or an existing customer.

Here's a simple diagram showing why every business needs a salє

Effect Of Positive Contacts In The Sales Cycle

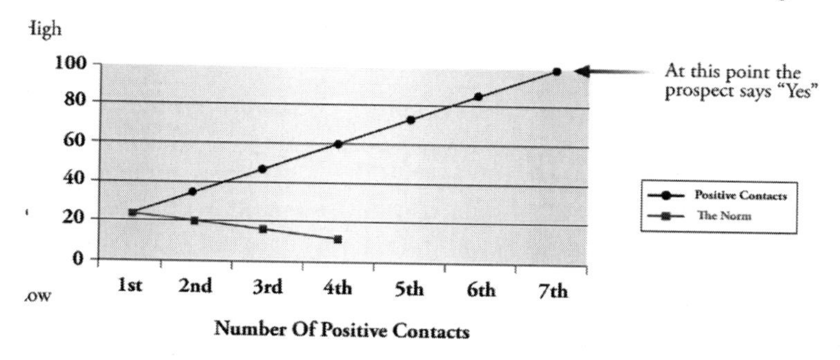

›rm – By the fourth contact the prospect's interest is lower than where it started.
:e now further away from the sale! That's why 90% of sales people have given up!

e Contacts – By the fourth contact the prospect's interest is high.
's only a matter of time and a couple more positive contacts before the sale is made.

What this diagram shows is that the prospect must reach a certain level of interest before he or she is prepared to say 'Yes' and buy your product or service.

Therefore, what you need to do is increase the prospect's interest each time the business makes contact with them. A contact can be a meeting (online or offline), a letter, an email, a phone call, an SMS text … or any way in which you make contact with prospects or, indeed, existing clients, customers or patients.

Did you know, for example, that, on average, it takes seven positive contacts (the 'Rule of 7') before the prospect says, 'Yes'. Using sales conversion, these steps are automatically built into the system, which increases the chances of getting a positive result with the vast majority of highly targeted prospects.

No matter what the business, there are several easily identifiable steps between the lead coming in and the prospect saying, 'yes'.

Your sales conversion system focuses on each stage, and, as a result, many more leads turn into sales.

But there's one more important piece of the jigsaw to consider; I call it the 'Follow-Up Ladder'. When you combine the Follow-Up Ladder with the 'Rule of 7', you have an unbeatable sales conversion system. Let me explain.

The Prospect Follow-Up Ladder (see next page – research conducted by Thomas Publishing and backed up by many more studies) explains the importance of following up and highlights the strong correlation between people buying on the seventh positive contact combined with the fact that most people give up on the prospect too early.

In other words, Follow-Up is not practised by many businesses. This means those that follow up correctly will always gain more customers.

When Do Prospects Turn Into Buyers?

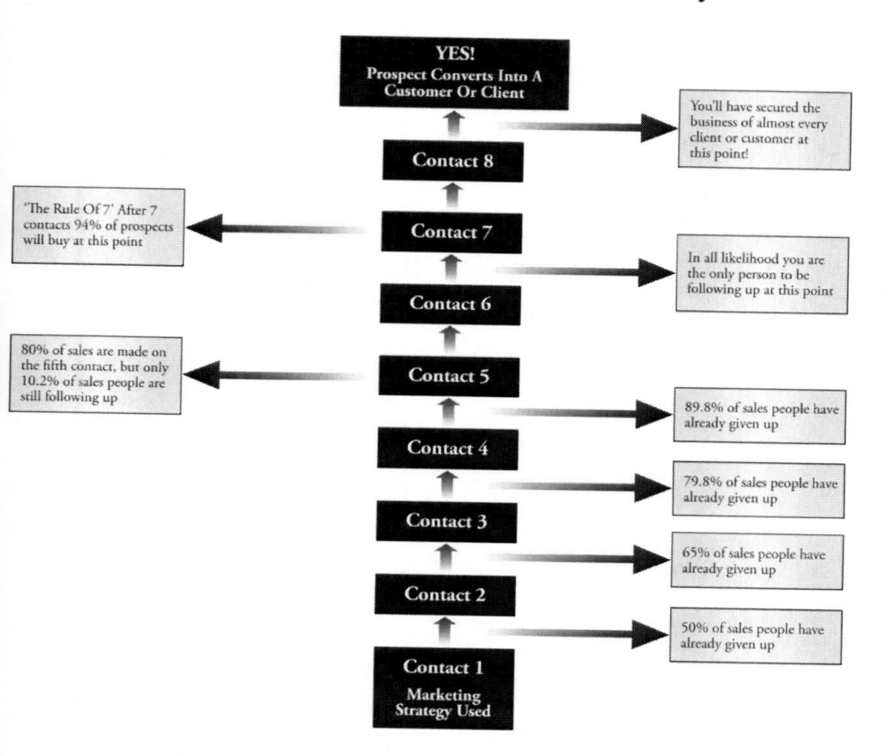

Data based on Thomas Publishing Company research findings

I also think you'll find these research results very interesting:

- A recent study conducted by Performark (a research company in the USA) showed how few companies follow up properly or even at all.

Performark found that, out of 10,000 advertising enquiries, 22% never received the information they requested, 45% received the information more than 65 days after their request, for 12% it took more than 120 days to receive their information, and 87% were never contacted by a sales representative.

- As shown in the previous diagram, a recent study by Thomas Publishing Company showed that most salespeople give up too early, regardless of the industry.

  According to the study, 80% of sales to business are made on the fifth sales call, but only 10% of salespeople call more than three times.

- A recent study conducted by Tom Rayfield, a UK direct marketing expert, showed that companies are very poor at follow-up. Taking 200 randomly selected advertisers, he replied to them all to measure follow-up responses.

  To his amazement, the average time taken for people to reply to him was eight days, and 17 companies (8.5%) didn't even bother to reply!

- Dr Geoffrey Lant, the renowned marketing and research consultant, reasons that most buying decisions are made after seven contacts over an 18-month period. He calls this the 'Rule of 7', and many more studies support this.

Having created hundreds of sales conversion systems over the years, I can tell you that all this information plays into your hands and ensures your sales conversion goes through the roof when you put your own system in place.

You need to make a positive impression on the prospect at each contact. By doing this, you speed up the sales cycle and keep more prospects interested, which results in more sales. Eventually, your persistent (but not too persistent that it pressures the prospect) communications make it difficult (in a good way!) for the prospect to refuse you.

If one of the steps in your sales conversion system has a less than positive impact on your prospect, their interest drops, making it harder for you to close the sale. This is a basic but very important tactic for you to apply and understand.

I'm going to take you through the exact steps you need to apply to your own business (and the logic behind it), so you can create your own winning sales conversion system. But first I just want to explain why so few businesses have any kind of system in place for converting more leads into sales.

There are four main reasons why:

- People are too busy working in their businesses to take time to develop a system.
- People simply aren't aware of the importance of a sales conversion system and what it can do for their sales, even though it makes total sense when I tell them about it (you don't know what you don't know).
- People focus only on generating leads from their marketing activity and are content with the number of leads that convert into customers – they don't realise how much business they're losing out on!

- People don't even know what their sales conversion rate is (the percentage of customers you get from the total number of enquiries received). But if you don't know what your conversion rate is, how can you go about improving it?

Here's why a sales conversion system is so powerful and why every business must have one.

Let's just take this hypothetical but very realistic situation.

Let's say, at the moment your business converts 20% of leads into sales. The average order is £1,000, and 10 leads are generated each month. Look at the table below and see the effect a sales conversion system can have on the business in just 12 months:

Conversion Rate	Leads Per Month	Sales Per Month	Average Order (£)	Annual Income (£)
20%	10	2	1000	24,000
30%	10	3	1000	36,000
40%	10	4	1000	48,000
50%	10	5	1000	60,000

Improving the sales conversion rate from 20% to 30% results in growth of 50%. Doubling the sales conversion rate from 20% to 40% results in 100% growth in new business. That's why a sales conversion process is so powerful and so important.

By the way, if you think it's difficult to transform your conversion from 20% to 40%, or 30% to 60%, or more – it isn't!

Of course, it depends on your industry, how the lead was generated and other factors, such as the competition, as to how high you can get your conversion. But just remember, whatever your conversion rate is at the moment, it can be better, and that will translate to a significant improvement in your sales and therefore profits.

For example, one of my private coaching clients, a general practice accounting firm, transformed their sales conversion rate from just under 20% to 90% in six short months. That's converting nine leads out of ten into clients as opposed to one in five. This isn't an isolated incident, although admittedly, it's rare to see conversion that high. But as I keep saying, all you have to know is that you CAN significantly transform your conversion when you put a system in place. Any improvement is worth it. Right?

And consider this:

Improving your sales conversion rate is achieved with very little increase in cost (if any).

The key to improving your sales conversion rate is first to find out what your sales conversion rate is at the moment (number of sales divided by number of leads and expressed as a percentage).

It will be different for each lead-generation strategy or tactic you're using, so work it out for each one, and then also calculate an average. Now you can get to work.

Let's now look at how you create a powerful sales conversion system for your business.

Creating a Sales Conversion System

STEP 1: Existing Sales Conversion Optimisation

If you haven't done so already, make sure you look at what's in place right now from the moment a lead is generated to it becoming a sale.

Of course, you need to review the Core Elements and make sure they are all being used and being used optimally. Although it is important to apply ALL the Core Elements, the following Core Elements will significantly contribute to increasing conversion:

- guarantee
- social Proof

This simple process of improving your existing conversion will enable you to get quick increases in sales without any extra expense.

STEP 2: Map the stages of the sales conversion system to create your Framework.

Use the Sales Conversion System Design Table shown on the next page. To make things even easier for you, you can download the actual document from here:

www.FreeFormulaBook.com/resources

Notice the very bottom row of the Framework is titled 'Maximise Customer Value System'. I'll explain how that follows in Chapter 7.

The Sales Conversion System Design Table

DAY	CONTACT	OBJECTIVE
LEAD GENERATED		
0		
STAGE 1: <Enter Details>		
0		
STAGE 2: <Enter Details>		
0		
STAGE 3: <Enter Details>		
0		
STAGE 4: <Enter Details>		
0		
SALE & NEW CUSTOMER ACQUIRED		
MAXIMISING CUSTOMER VALUE SYSTEM		

Simply use the table to first map the key STAGES that have to occur as part of your sales process. A stage could be any of the following:

- a meeting
- a form received
- a visit to the store
- etc.

The system starts the moment the lead is generated and ends when the sale is made. By adding the key stages between these two points, you've created the 'Framework'.

You may even find it easier to get a sheet of paper, turn it so it's landscape, then draw a horizontal line from the left to the right. On the far left write 'Lead Generated', and on the far right, write 'Sale'.

You may have any number of stages. Simply include all of them in the 'Stages' rows in chronological order in the Sales Conversion Design Table.

Let's say I run an accounting firm; my key stages would be:

- meeting arranged
- reception greeting
- the meeting
- post-meeting

Here's how that looks in my table:

The Sales Conversion System Design Table – With Stages Entered

DAY	CONTACT	OBJECTIVE
	LEAD GENERATED	
0		
	STAGE 1: Meeting Arranged	
0		
	STAGE 2: Reception Greeting	
0		
	STAGE 3: The Meeting	
0		
	STAGE 4: Post Meeting	
0		
	SALE & NEW CUSTOMER ACQUIRED	
	MAXIMISING CUSTOMER VALUE SYSTEM	

STEP 3: Decide how many contacts you require.

Now you have your Framework in place, you need to decide on the number of contacts between each of the stages.

As a guide, the higher the price of your product or service and/or the longer the sales cycle (i.e. the average time it takes for a prospect to move to the next Stage), the more contacts you'll want to build in.

Your contacts go in the 'Contact' column of the Design table.

Using my example of an accounting firm, here are the contacts I would include:

Lead generated

- Receive inbound phone call or make out-bound call (depending on how the lead was generated).
- Partner speaks to prospect.

Please Note: It's very important at this stage to make sure that when the initial lead comes in, you collect any other additional details from the prospect. If you're going to use email, SMS texts and mail, for example, you must get the email address, mobile number and postal address of the prospect.

STAGE 1: Meeting arranged

- Email details of meeting (send agenda, directions and parking instructions).
- Send confirmation letter.
- Send 'Surprise Package' prior to meeting (this may include video testimonials, a couple of special reports and a welcome video from the partner further introducing him or herself to the prospect and telling them they are looking forward to the meeting).

STAGE 2: Reception greeting

- Receptionist greets prospect when they arrive.
- Offer refreshments (use 'Drinks Menu').
- Partner also greets prospect in person.

STAGE 3: The meeting

- Follow meeting sales process (use multiple presentation aids).
- Ask for the order.

STAGE 4: Post-meeting

- Meeting follow-up letter
- Phone call
- Follow-up system

Notice that because you're now taking a strategic approach to your sales conversion, you can add elements you believe will enhance the prospect journey from lead to customer. Think about the contacts you can add that will have a positive effect on the prospect.

Here's how this now looks in my table:

The Sales Conversion Design Table – With Stages and Contacts Entered

DAY	CONTACT	OBJECTIVE
LEAD GENERATED		
0	Receive in-bound call (or make out-bound call)	
	Partner speaks with prospect	
STAGE 1: Meeting Arranged		
0	Email details of meeting	
	Send confirmation letter	
	Send Surprise Package	
STAGE 2: Reception Greeting		
0	Receptionist greets prospect	
	Offer refreshments	
	Partner greets prospect	
STAGE 3: The Meeting		
0	Follow meeting sales process	
	Ask for the order	
STAGE 4: Post Meeting		
0	Meeting follow-up letter	
	Follow-up phone call	
	Follow-up system	
SALE & NEW CUSTOMER ACQUIRED		
MAXIMISING CUSTOMER VALUE SYSTEM		

STEP 4: Write down the objective of each contact.

This is imperative. Every contact has to have an objective. There are two types of objectives you need to think about:

1. Courtesy objectives: For example, thanking the prospect and informing them of what will happen next.

   Here's an email you could send:

   ```
   Subject: Thank you, John

   Hi John,

   I just wanted to say thank you for
   requesting our brochure. I'll send you
   a quick email to let you know when
   we've despatched it.

   Look out for the Introductory Special
   Offer on page 5.

   Thanks again, John.

   Kind regards,

   Dave Jones
   Managing Director
   ```

2. Next step objectives. For example, the covering letter with the brochure has the objective of getting the prospect to request a meeting.

   Having already constructed your Framework (made up from each stage), the objective is easy. It is simply to get the prospect to reach the next stage in your sales conversion system.

   Add the objective to the table in the 'Objective Column'.

STEP 5: Add Timeline

Now, for each contact, simply decide on when the contact will occur. Day 0 means the contact happens the same day as the Critical Stage is reached. Day 3 means the contact is delivered three days after the stage was reached, and so on.

Once a Critical Stage is reached the timeline starts again at zero.

STEP 6: Decide the exact nature of each contact and create.

Decide what each contact will consist of.

What will you include?

What will you say?

For example, my initial confirmation email, may look something like this:

```
Subject: Our meeting …

Good afternoon, Julie.

I'm just writing to confirm our meeting at our
offices on 21 November at 10 a.m.

I have also written to you today with further
details including an Agenda and directions.

If you have any questions before our meeting
please email me on:

>> steve@abcaccountants.com

… or call me on <Telephone Number>.
```

```
Thanks again, Julie. I'm looking forward to
meeting you.

Kind regards,

Steve Hackney
Partner
```

STEP 7: Add the Core Elements where you can.

Steps 1–6 take you through the procedure you need to follow to put your actual sales conversion system (sales process) in place.

Now you're going to look at each contact and add, where relevant, as many of the Core Elements as you can.

The more you add, the higher your conversion will be.

For example, if you need some kind of sales meeting, then make sure you have a list of social proof to show the prospect, add a powerful guarantee and give them an offer they can't refuse.

Trust me, when you add the power of the Core Elements and sprinkle them throughout your sales conversion system, you're going to enjoy results like you've never seen before.

STEP 8: Keep following up to take advantage of 'the moving parade'.

Selling any product or service is all about timing. Just because someone isn't interested in buying your product or service today, it doesn't mean they aren't going to be interested tomorrow.

That is, in essence, what 'The Moving Parade' is all about. Let me explain this further.

Let's say that at the moment you're really happy with your car. You've got no intention of changing it. Therefore, every advert, every mailing or any contact you have with a car dealer or car manufacturer is wasted on you.

Letters go in the bin without a second thought. You pick up your newspaper when the adverts come on TV. You simply aren't interested. And nothing will prompt you at this stage to even consider changing your car.

However, three months later your circumstances have changed. You need to do more travelling, and so you decide it's time to look for a more suitable car.

Now, every mailing, advert or communication to do with cars is instantly given attention by you. You're 'in the market' for a new car, and you develop an insatiable appetite to find out as much as you can about the cars which would suit you best.

This happens every single day when people are buying products and services.

If you don't keep in touch regularly with your prospects and customers, you'll never get 'lucky' with the timing. People move in and out of the market, depending on changing circumstances – The Moving Parade (see diagram on the next page).

By keeping in contact at least once a month, the chances that you will hit the prospect at the right time are increased tenfold. You will get 'LUCKY'!

The Moving Parade – What It Looks Like

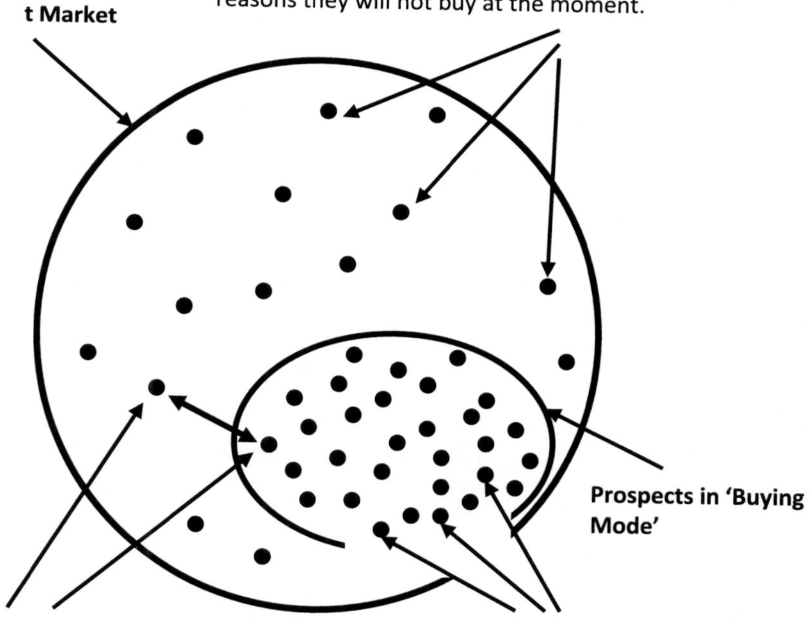
These people outside the 'Buying Mode' circle are in your target market or niche, but for a number of reasons they will not buy at the moment.
t Market
Prospects in 'Buying Mode'

Moving Parade:
ple/Businesses That Either
ɔme Buyers or Non-Buyers

ɔle or businesses move in and
of 'buying mode' all the time.
ɹmstances change, resulting
ɘople or businesses either
ɔming buyers or non-buyers.
movement in and out of
ing mode' is what we call The
'ing Parade.

ple/Businesses Who Are
ɖy to Buy Right Now

ɕe people inside the 'Buying
le' circle are ready to buy
: now. Remember, they can
buy from YOU or your
petitors.

g a range of stand-out
keting pieces helps you win a
ɘ proportion of these
omers.

Do this one thing, and your sales and profits will increase. Do NOT take this lightly. Taking advantage of The Moving Parade is one of the simplest yet most rewarding marketing strategies you can apply to any business.

By far the easiest thing to send every month is your Monthly Printed Newsletter (see Chapter 7)!

Step 9: Monitor, test and improve

Once your sales conversion system is operating, you can measure, test and improve the results of each contact.

Key to this is maybe adding or removing certain contacts within each stage and making sure you're optimising all the Core Elements, where relevant.

Conclusion:

This is probably the first time you've been shown anything like this when it comes to converting leads into sales. Believe me, this is extremely powerful and costs very little to put in place.

Even if you have a short sales cycle, you'll be able to build in great contacts that demonstrate to the prospect that you would be a great business to buy from (or keep buying from).

This may seem to be a complex system to put in place, but don't worry. I'll deal with this in Chapter 8, when I talk to you about systems and automation.

Okay. You've transformed all your existing sales and marketing tactics and strategies. You've added your lead generation-strategies and created a highly successful sales conversion system. Now let's look at the most lucrative part of your business, one that in my experience is neglected by almost every small and medium sized business: maximising the value of your clients, customers or patients…

Chapter Summary

- Concentrating on converting more leads into clients, customers, or patients will ensure two things:

    1. You'll transform your business overnight
    2. You'll maximise the investment (time and money) you make on all your lead generation strategies

- Conversion is one of the key leverage points in your business – one where you can make quick and instant gains.

- A sales conversion system is a set of logical steps from the moment a lead is generated, to the moment a sale is made, with the sole goal being to generate as many good quality sales as possible.

- On average, it takes 7 positive contacts before the Prospect says 'Yes'. Those that combine 7 positive contacts in their follow-up as part of their sales conversion system will always gain more clients, customers or patients.

Creating A Sales Conversion System

Step 1: Existing sales conversion optimisation

Step 2: Map the stages of the sales conversion system to create your Framework.

Step 3: Decide how many contacts you require

Step 4: Write down the objective of each contact (2 types of objectives: Courtesy Objectives and Next Step Objectives)

Step 5: Add Timeline

Step 6: Decide the exact nature of each contact and create it

Step 7: Add the Core Elements where you can

Step 8: Keep following up to take advantage of the 'Moving Parade'

Step 9: Monitor, test and improve.

CHAPTER 7:

MAXIMISING CUSTOMER VALUE

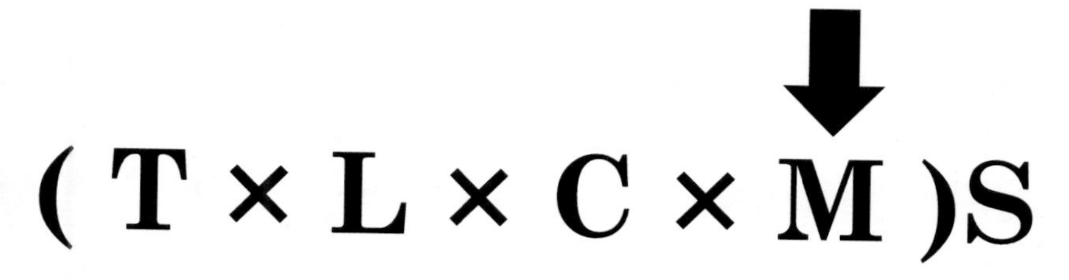

= EXPONENTIAL BUSINESS GROWTH

y coaches and I can go into almost any business and find thousands of pounds of revenue and profit, literally overnight. We can do this not because we're some kind of magicians, but because we can tap into the often ignored but highly lucrative part of a business that I call its *Acres of Diamonds*.

Every business on the planet possesses this.

What are 'Acres of Diamonds', I hear you ask?

Let me explain with a true story.

One of the most interesting Americans who lived in the nineteenth century was a man by the name of Russell Herman Conwell. He was born in 1843 and lived until 1925. He was a lawyer for about 15 years until he became a clergyman.

One day, a young man went to him and told him he wanted a college education but couldn't swing it financially. Dr. Conwell decided, at that moment, what his aim in life was – besides being a man of the cloth, that is. He decided to build a university for unfortunate but deserving students. He did have a challenge, however. He would need a few million dollars to build the university. For Dr. Conwell, and anyone with real purpose in life, nothing could stand in the way of his goal.

Several years before this incident, Dr. Conwell was tremendously intrigued by a true story with an ageless moral. The story was about a farmer who lived in Africa and through a visitor became tremendously excited about looking for diamonds.

Diamonds had already been discovered in abundance on the African continent and this farmer got so excited about the idea of millions of dollars' worth of diamonds that he sold his farm to head out to the diamond line.

He wandered all over the continent, as the years slipped by, constantly searching for diamonds and wealth, which he never found. Eventually, he went completely broke and threw himself into a river and drowned.

Meanwhile, the new owner of his farm picked up an unusual looking rock about the size of a country egg and put it on his mantle as a sort of curiosity.

A visitor stopped by and, seeing the rock, practically went into terminal convulsions.

He told the new owner of the farm that the funny-looking rock on his mantle was about the biggest diamond that had ever been found. The new owner of the farm said, 'Heck, the whole farm is covered with them', and, sure enough, it was.

The farm turned out to be the Kimberley Diamond Mine, the richest the world has ever known. The original farmer was literally standing on 'Acres of Diamonds' until he sold his farm.

Dr. Conwell learned from the story of the farmer and continued to teach its moral. Each of us is right in the middle of our own 'Acre of Diamonds', if only we would realise it and develop the ground we are standing on before charging off in search of greener pastures.

Dr. Conwell told this story many times and attracted enormous audiences. He told the story long enough to raise the money to start the college for underprivileged deserving students. In fact, he raised nearly six million dollars, and the university he founded, Temple University in Philadelphia, has at least 10 degree-granting colleges and six other schools.

When Doctor Russell H. Conwell talked about each of us being right on our own 'Acre of Diamonds', he meant it. This story does not get old; it will be true forever. Opportunity does not just come along; it is there all the time. We just have to see it.

So how does this relate to you and the business? Any ideas?

Well, by far and away the most lucrative part of any business is its customers.

It's the customers who are your own 'Acres of Diamonds'.

Once a new client, customer or patient is acquired, it's your duty to enrich their life by giving them more value: more services; more products; more benefits.

This is known as 'Back-End Selling', and when this is carried out successfully (it isn't hard when you know how!), you'll release so much cash for the business, you'll wonder what to do with it. Therefore, the Maximising Customer Value part of THE FORMULA focuses on **increasing the value of each customer**.

There are four key areas that will help you to do that:

1. **Increase the frequency of purchase** (getting clients, customers or patients to buy more often).
2. **Increase referrals** (getting clients, customers or patients to recommend you more often).
3. **Increase average order value** (increasing the value of every sale).
4. **Reduce attrition** (keeping hold of clients, customers or patients for longer).

You MUST use strategies across all four of these areas, and I'll come on to this shortly. Without doubt this is the most neglected part of virtually every small or medium sized business.

Yet, as I've said, your customer list is one of the most valuable assets your business will ever have. In other words, there's ***G-O-L-D*** in your customer list. You just need to learn how to extract it and what follows will explain exactly how you can do exactly that!

In fact, there are at least 11 proven low- or zero-cost strategies that you can use right now that will have an incredible effect on your success. For example:

- Moments of Truth (see later)
- Monthly Customer Prize Draw
- Customer Penetration System (see later)
- Customer Offer of the Month
- Up-Sell (see later)
- Cross-Sell (see later)
- Reactivate Past Customers
- Referral System (see later)
- Customer Welcome Letter
- Dealing with Complaints
- Monthly Customer Newsletter (see later)

Better, still, just like we did with the Conversion part of THE FORMULA, you're going to create a system.

Let's take a look at how you put your own Maximising Customer Value System together.

Creating Your Maximising Customer Value System

STEP 1: Transform existing tactics and strategies

If you haven't done so already, make sure you've optimised and transformed your existing maximising customer value tactics and strategies.

This will enable you to get quick increases in sales from existing customers without any extra expense.

You're looking at everything you do once the customer has been acquired. If you recall the Sales Conversion System Design Table in Chapter 6, the last entry at the bottom of the table is the 'Maximising Customer Value System'. It kicks in immediately after the client, customer or patient has been acquired.

So what do you currently do?

Take everything – and I mean *everything* – and use the Core Elements, where relevant, to improve each contact you have with your clients, customers or patients.

If you're running a start-up or new business, and you don't yet have customers, jump to step 2.

STEP 2: Use Moments of Truth to build an amazing customer experience.

Your investment in this book is worth this single step alone.

In 1987 Jan Carlzon, the CEO of Scandinavian Airlines, wrote the book, *Moments of Truth*. It explained how he took the airline from deficit to profit by 'moving' the airline to a customer-focused organisation.

Now, as you know, there have been many books written on customer service, but where this book and Carlzon's strategies really differ is his focus on each interaction the customer has with the business.

He calls these ***Moments of Truth***, and, of course, each interaction can be a positive or a negative experience.

Take a look at the diagram on the next page. It shows how, at each contact (Moment of Truth), you need to ensure each interaction is a favourable one for the customer.

Scandinavian Airlines prospered because they worked very hard to make sure each Moment of Truth with their customers was a very positive experience, and the results they achieved were a testament to this.

Therefore, what you need to do is increase the satisfaction level of each customer when any contact occurs (Moment of Truth).

As previously, when we looked at creating your sales conversion system, a contact can be a meeting (online or offline), a letter/postcard, etc., an SMS text, email, telephone call ... or any way in which your business comes into contact with a customer.

So how can you use this to your advantage? There are just a couple of simple steps. Let's take a look at each one.

#1: Write down all possible interactions (moments) you have with your customers.

This is simple. Here's what you do.

Moments of Truth Explained

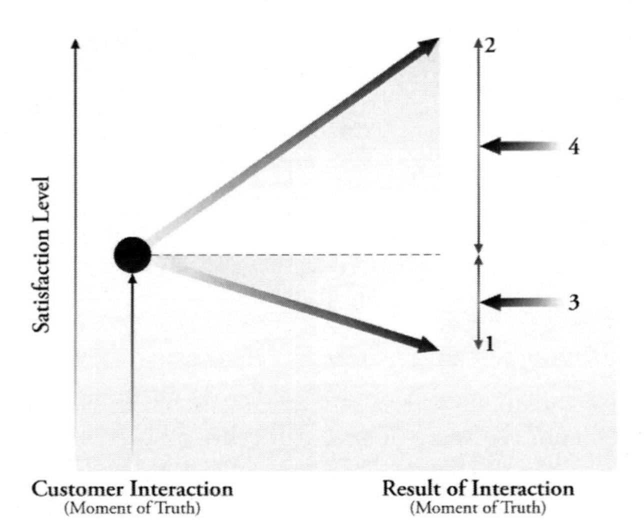

Legend

1. The effect on the customer when the business doesn't actively focus on each interaction with its customers. Notice the Moment of Truth was a negative experience, reducing the customer's satisfaction and therefore creating discontent (no matter how small).
2. Moments of Truth Approach. By breaking down each point of contact to ensure excellent customer experience, the interest and satisfaction level is raised even higher.
3. Shows the drop in interest level and satisfaction when a business doesn't focus on each point of contact.
4. Shows the increase gained by using Moments of Truth techniques.

Use the Moments of Truth Design Table (see next page) and firstly, identify every single interaction you have with your customers and enter them in the Moment of Truth column – every single one. Write these in chronological order (where possible).

Then, for each section, make sure you enter *when* the moment will happen and the detail of *what* you'll be doing to make it a positive experience for the customer.

Notice there are four sections.

Section 1: Customer Acquired – Immediate Moments (in here, write down exactly what happens the moment you get a customer).

Let's say, for example, I'm running a domestic plumbing business. This is what I'd enter in section 1:

- Email summarising the order and confirming the time and date the plumber will be arriving at their home

Section 2: Product/Service Delivery Moments (in here, write down the points of contact as you deliver your product or service to the customer).

Using my example of a domestic plumbing business, in this section I'd write:

- Arrive on time.
- Carry out job as per the spec sheet.

Moments of Truth Design Table

MOMENT OF TRUTH	WHEN
CUSTOMER ACQUIRED – IMMEDIATE MOMENTS	
PRODCUT/SERVICE DELIVERY MOMENTS	
ONGOING MOMENTS	
SPECIAL MOMENTS	
WORLD-CLASS CUSTOMER EXPERIENCE	

Please Note: You can download the document from here:

www.FreeFormulaBook.com/resources

Section 3: Ongoing Moments (in here, write down the things you're going to do to keep in touch with the customer).

Here's what I'd write in this section for my example:

- Doing nothing at the moment (leave blank)

Section 4: Special Moments (in here, write down things you're going to do that will WOW the customer).

Please Note: In the first three sections you've added only the basics. This is the minimum level of interaction you should be having with your customers (this is normal, most businesses don't do what we're about to do next).

Without question, when you adopt Moments of Truth, you'll be adding so much more to each section. We do this with *Special Moments of Truth*. For example, here's what I'd add:

Section 1 – Special Moments:

- Send SMS text to let customer know plumber will be arriving within 30 minutes.

Section 2 – Special Moments:

- Plumber to arrive 10 minutes early.
- Plumber to knock on door and greet customer politely.
- Prior to entering house, put on floor protector bags around each boot.
- Work tidily always (use personal hand vacuum cleaner to keep dirt and mess to a minimum).
- Prior to leaving job, explain to customer what's been done, get them to check work is to their satisfaction and complete 'Job Sign Off Sheet'.

- Before leaving, deliver 'Promotion leaflet' to six houses to the left, six houses to the right and 12 over the road (if applicable).

Section 3 – Special Moments:

- Send our monthly printed newsletter.

See the next page for my completed Moments of Truth Design Table.

This is NOT rocket science. We all instinctively know what will make people think 'WOW', because we're all customers of many other businesses. We can also count on one hand how many businesses we've bought from, when we think 'WOW'.

I've got a good example to share with you here. It's a WOW Moment of Truth we introduced when we ran our franchise consultancy business.

New clients (the franchisors) were invited for a full day at our headquarters for them to meet the team and for us to put the complete plan in place for developing their franchise.

It was an amazing day full of great Moments of Truth. We'd take them for lunch and treat them like royalty throughout.

But the one thing they were most appreciative of (even though the entire day was about giving them the vision for their franchise) was when they left the building and walked to their car: we'd had the outside of their car valeted!

My Completed Moments of Truth Design Table

MOMENT OF TRUTH	*WHEN*
CUSTOMER ACQUIRED – IMMEDIATE MOMENTS	
Email summarising order and confirming time and date the plumber will arrive at their home	Immediately
Send SMS text to let customer know plumber will be arriving within 30 minutes	30 minutes prior to plumber arriving
PRODUCT/SERVICE DELIVERY MOMENTS	
Plumber to arrive 10 minutes early	At customers house
Carry out job as per spec sheet	
Plumber to knock on door and greet customer politely	
Prior to entering house, put on floor protector bags around each boot	
Work tidily always (use personal hand vacuum cleaner to keep dirt and mess to a minimum)	
Prior to leaving job, explain to customer what's been done, get them to check work is to their satisfaction and complete 'Job Sign Off Sheet'	
Before leaving, deliver 'Promotion leaflet' to 6 houses to the left, 6 houses to the right and 12 over the road (if applicable)	
ONGOING MOMENTS	
Send our monthly printed newsletter	Every month
SPECIAL MOMENTS	
I've moved my Special Moments Of Truth up to the relevant sections above	
You'll add additional Special Moments Of Truth on an ongoing basis	
WORLD-CLASS CUSTOMER EXPERIENCE	

Once the car had been valeted, we put a waterproof envelope under their windscreen wiper, and inside was a simple card personally addressed to them and signed by the team saying:

> 'Hi Carole, we hope you had a wonderful day today. As a thank you for taking the time to meet with us, we've valeted the outside of your car for you. Have a safe journey home'.

That whole experience cost us around £15, but it was worth every single penny.

It was a member of the team that came up with that WOW Moment of Truth, which leads me nicely on to the next point.

If you have staff, get them involved in this stage. They'll have a huge amount of ideas on how to create a WOW experience for the customer right across these three sections of customer interaction.

Get staff to 'own' this part of the process, and you'll be staggered how good your Moments of Truth will become.

#2: Create and systemise the positive experience at each moment.

Now simply prepare and create each moment to maximise the interaction so your customers have a positive experience with you at each one.

For example:

Let's say you have periodic meetings with your customers. Each meeting is, of course, a Moment of Truth.

You need to break down each phase of the meeting right from the moment the customer walks through your door to the moment they leave.

What happens as they enter your offices? Who greets them? What do they say? What drinks will be provided? Etc. All these things are very important and will make a significant difference to the 'experience' the customer has.

In effect, you're systemising the whole Moment of Truth to ensure the best possible outcome.

Another great example of Moments of Truth

Just in case you have any doubts about the power of Moments of Truth and the effect they can have on your business, here's a great example of how any industry can capitalise on this fabulous tactic.

Harvey Mackay (author of *Swim with the Sharks Without Being Eaten Alive*), tells a wonderful story about a cab driver that demonstrates Moments of Truth perfectly.

Harvey was waiting in line for a ride at the airport.

When a cab pulled up, the first thing Harvey noticed was that the taxi was polished to a bright shine.

Smartly dressed in a white shirt, black tie and freshly pressed black slacks, the cab driver jumped out and rounded the car to open the back passenger door for Harvey.

He handed Harvey a laminated card and said:

'I'm Wally, your driver. While I'm loading your bags in the trunk, I'd like you to read my mission statement.'

Taken aback, Harvey read the card. It said: Wally's Mission Statement:

To get my customers to their destination in the quickest, safest and cheapest way possible in a friendly environment.

This blew Harvey away, especially when he noticed that the inside of the cab matched the outside: spotlessly clean!

As he slid behind the wheel, Wally said, 'Would you like a cup of coffee? I have a thermos of regular and one of decaf.'

Harvey said jokingly, 'No, I'd prefer a soft drink.'

Wally smiled and said, 'No problem. I have a cooler up front with regular and Diet Coke, water and orange juice.'

Almost stuttering, Harvey said, 'I'll take a Diet Coke.'

Handing him his drink, Wally said, 'If you'd like something to read, I have the *Wall Street Journal*, *Time*, *Sports Illustrated* and *USA Today*.'

As they were pulling away, Wally handed Harvey another laminated card.

'These are the stations I get and the music they play if you'd like to listen to the radio.'

And, as if that were not enough, Wally told Harvey that he had the air conditioning on and asked if the temperature was comfortable for him.

Then he advised Harvey of the best route to his destination for that time of day.

He also let him know that he'd be happy to chat and tell him about some of the sights or, if Harvey preferred, to leave him with his own thoughts.

Then Harvey said, 'Tell me, Wally, have you always served customers like this?'

Wally smiled into the rear-view mirror. 'No, not always. In fact, it's only been in the last two years. My first five years driving, I spent most of my time complaining like all the rest of the cabbies do.

'Then I decided to do things differently. I looked around at the other cabs and their drivers. The cabs were dirty, the drivers were unfriendly, and the customers were unhappy. So I decided to make some changes. I put in a few at a time. When my customers responded, well, I did more.'

'I take it that has paid off for you,' Harvey said.

'It sure has,' Wally replied. 'In my first year, I doubled my income from the previous year. This year I'll probably quadruple it. You were lucky to get me today. I don't sit at cabstands anymore.

'My customers call me for appointments on my cell phone or leave a message on my answering machine. If I can't pick them up myself, I get a reliable cabbie friend to do it, and I take a piece of the action.'

Wally was implementing Moments of Truth, even though he didn't realise it!

This true story shows if Moments of Truth can be so successful for a cab driver, it can work for any type of business!

STEP 3: Create and activate at least one maximising tactic and strategy for each of the four customer maximisation areas.

It is essential that you have at least one tactic and strategy for each of the following four areas of maximising customer value;

1. **Increase the frequency of purchase** (getting clients, customers or patients to buy more often).
2. **Increase referrals** (getting clients, customers or patients to recommend you more often).
3. **Increase average order value** (increasing the value of every sale).
4. **Reduce attrition** (keeping hold of clients, customers or patients for longer).

As I mentioned earlier, it's also important you implement each tactic or strategy as quickly as you can, to ensure you maximise your results to the full.

This is a very exciting part of building your business. There are so many easy tactics and strategies you can add.

The good news is that you've already added Moments of Truth, which is great, because it has a major effect on all four areas above.

So, what I'm going to do now is to take you through one of my favourite strategies for each of the four areas, starting with 'Increasing The Frequency of Purchase'.

The Customer Penetration System

This is a simple but ingenious way to increase the frequency of purchase. I learned this some time ago from Peter Thomson, the great UK business strategist.

It focusses on the fact that most businesses are very poor at communicating what products and services they sell. Consequently, if customers don't know what products and services a business sells, they are less likely to even consider buying them, even if they want them.

Often what happens is that a customer will use another supplier of that product or service, not because they didn't want to buy from the business who originally sold to them, but because they were completely unaware that they could buy that product or service from them.

It's been proved that the more you educate customers about your products and services, the more sales you'll make. Simple!

Take a look at the spreadsheet below showing the Customer Penetration System. You can obviously use your CRM (customer relationship management system) to do this, but the spreadsheet on the next page shows you how it works.

Customer Penetration System

	Products/Services					
Customer Names	**1**	**2**	**3**	**4**	**5**	**Product Penetration %**
<Enter Name>						20
<Enter Name>						20
<Enter Name>						20
<Enter Name>						20
<Enter Name>						60
<Enter Name>						20
<Enter Name>						20
<Enter Name>						40
<Enter Name>						40
<Enter Name>						20
Customer Penetration %	30	10	40	20	30	

Let me explain how you use it.

- Across the top you list your products and/or services. In this example, there are five products.
- Along the side you list all your clients, customers or patients.

- If a customer has purchased a product or service, the box is completely filled in. So **customer 10 has purchased product 4**.
- The bottom of the box is filled in if the customer has been sent an offer on that particular product or service. So, in our example, **customer 1** has had an **offer sent on product 2**, but has not yet bought.
- The far-right column (Product Penetration) shows the percentage of products purchased by each customer. So **customer 5 has a 60% product penetration**.
- The bottom row (Customer Penetration) shows the percentage of customers who have bought each individual product or service. So **40% of customers have purchased product 3**.
- Once you've completed the spreadsheet, you'll see some massive gaps that need filling.
- Start by creating offers around each product and service, and communicate these offers to each customer (who hasn't bought that particular product or service yet).
- Each month, customers should be receiving information and offers on at least one of your products or services.

You're probably thinking, well that just seems too easy; too straightforward.

And you'd be right.

But don't dismiss it because of its simplicity.

THE FORMULA

Often, it's the simplest things that work well, and in all the years I've been using Peter's ingenious system (he calls it the 'Magic Matrix'), it always works, because, as I've said, most people take for granted that their customers know exactly what they offer, but the reality couldn't be further from the truth.

Key to the whole strategy then is to create irresistible customer offers each month. Here's an example of a very successful one you can use and adapt.

It's from the eyewear industry. This offer letter was sent to existing customers in an effort to sell off excess stock. Within seven days the entire stock was snapped up by existing customers.

Here's why it worked so well:

1. When the offer is strong, it's so easy just to lead with it in the headline.
2. The opening is a proven way to start any letter, on the proviso that your letter is going to be short and to the point!
3. Communication of the offer in full.
4. Scarcity is important with all your offers. What you want to do is reduce procrastination. The more specific you are, the better. As I mentioned above, this offer actually sold out in just under seven days (not 10 as I initially thought).
5. Strong call to action.

Buy Three Atlas Frames
And Get One FREE

Good Morning <FirstName>,

This letter is going to be short and to the point.

Buy any three Atlas frames and get **one FREE**. That's it. No strings. All I ask is you choose your FREE Atlas frames from models A6, A7, A8, A9 and A13 (please see your Olympus Brochure).

We're getting to the end of the year, and I've just finished doing my annual stock take. The children's models A6-A9 and A13 are surplus stock. Just buy any three Atlas frames, and choose your FREE frame from these five models. By the way, this offer is only available to our current customers!

There are only 694 FREE frames available. I expect to sell out within the next 10 days - so you'll have to be quick to take advantage!

Call us now on **<Number>**, or speak to your Olympus Sales Agent. Alternatively, complete the 'Urgent Fax Back Form' enclosed, and fax it to us on **<Number>**.

Thank you for your continued business.

Kind regards

<Full Name>
<Title>

```
P.S. Remember this offer is only available
while stocks last. Call us now on <Number>.
```

IMPORTANT:

I've found when you're doing any type of offer to clients, customers or patients that you will maximise results by using several different media. So, for example, send letters, emails and texts. Make sure, within reason, you communicate the offer several times (at least three times).

It's never good enough to send just one email or just one letter. And don't restrict yourself to using only email because it's easy and cheap. I promise that if you mix in direct mail (letters, postcards, etc.) with your online media, your results will literally multiply.

Oh … and before I forget, NEVER address your client, customer or patient as 'Dear Valued Client' or something similar. Make sure you use their name, otherwise your results will bomb!

Now let's look at the second area of maximising customer value and increasing referrals'…

The Referral System

Many people fail to ask for referrals from existing clients, customers or patients. Just hoping and waiting for their best customers to refer friends, colleagues and business associates isn't good enough.

That approach is what I call 'passive'.

Other than provide a good product or service, you're hoping that will translate into goodwill, and that customers will refer others to you.

Of course, every good business gets referrals, but if I told you that with very little additional cost you could multiply the referrals you get by a factor of 5 or 10, would you be interested?

Well that's exactly what will happen when you put in place a *referral system*.

Putting in place a referral system that focuses on getting referrals is one of the easiest and most rewarding things you can do.

A structured referral system will give your business the following benefits:

- A constant supply of quality referrals.
- Increased enthusiasm dealing with people who are highly interested in your product or service.
- An increase in the quality of clients, customers or patients.
- Increased profits. You spend less time and money converting referred people. They have already been recommended, and therefore trust is already established.
- As a result, referred people tend to value the product or service more than an 'ordinary' prospect. They usually don't 'shop around' to get the best price. This means you'll be able to sell your product or service at an optimum price.

- A referral system will help strengthen relationships with customers. By helping their friends, colleagues and business associates, you make customers look good in the eyes of the referred party.

Rules to remember when adopting a referral system

Although your referral system will be quick and easy to implement, you must adhere to the following 'rules' if you want your system to work effectively.

1. One major fault with many people who ask for referrals is that they don't stress to the customer the benefits they receive from doing business with them.

   You must constantly inform and re-educate customers about why doing business with you is beneficial to them. Once they understand and accept these benefits, they are **primed to give you good referrals**.

2. Always write or call and thank the customer for the referral. Let them know how you got on with the referred person, even if it doesn't result in any business. Keeping in touch in this way is very important.

3. Make sure you offer an incentive. This one thing puts your referral system on steroids and will multiply results. It doesn't have to be a cash incentive (unless your referral system is based on monetary rewards). Tickets to a sporting occasion, the opera, cinema, a donation to their favourite charity, or anything that the customer values, are excellent ways of rewarding them. Remember, it doesn't cost you to acquire a referred client, customer or patient, so you can afford to give an

incentive. Don't be tight. The bigger and better the incentive, the more referrals you'll get. Fact!

4. Make sure **all** staff are aware of the referral system you are adopting. Staff can also be an excellent source of referrals. Most of the time they need educating on the benefits of referrals to the business. You can also incentivise staff for producing referrals (non-sales staff, of course).

5. Even if a referred person doesn't initially become a customer, you must keep communicating with them. Keep them interested by sending information that's useful to them (sending them your monthly printed newsletter is a great way to do this).

   In time, many will convert into customers.

Transform your business into a referral 'machine'

You'll find it relatively easy to put a referral system in place. Choose your incentive, communicate the referral system regularly, and you're on your way. Results will be good, but you can improve them significantly by immersing the business in the referral system.

Here's what I mean:

Your referral system will help to create a constant stream of referrals, but that's not good enough.

Sure, it will bring you many more new clients than ever before, but you turbo-charge your referral system by INTEGRATING it completely into your business. This is when you create your own 'Referral Mushroom', and your business transforms into a 'referral-based business'! The diagram on the next page shows you exactly what I mean by this, and what you should do.

So, let's look at what you need to do to integrate the system completely into your firm.

Add to all agendas

If you don't use agendas in your meetings (either face-to-face or by telephone), you're missing a huge opportunity in many different ways.

The last item of your agenda should always be a reinforcement of your referral system.

When you get to this point in the agenda, reiterate to them what your referral system involves (depending on the incentive you've chosen) and explain to them what they get as a result of a referral that converts into a client, customer or patient. Tell them that your best customers are always referred ones, and that's why you invest so much time and effort in your referral programme.

Add to all emails

Reinforce your key referral message in your email signature by adding your referral incentive.

Add to bills/invoices

Another great place to reinforce your referral system is at the bottom of all your bills/invoices.

The 'Mushroom Effect'

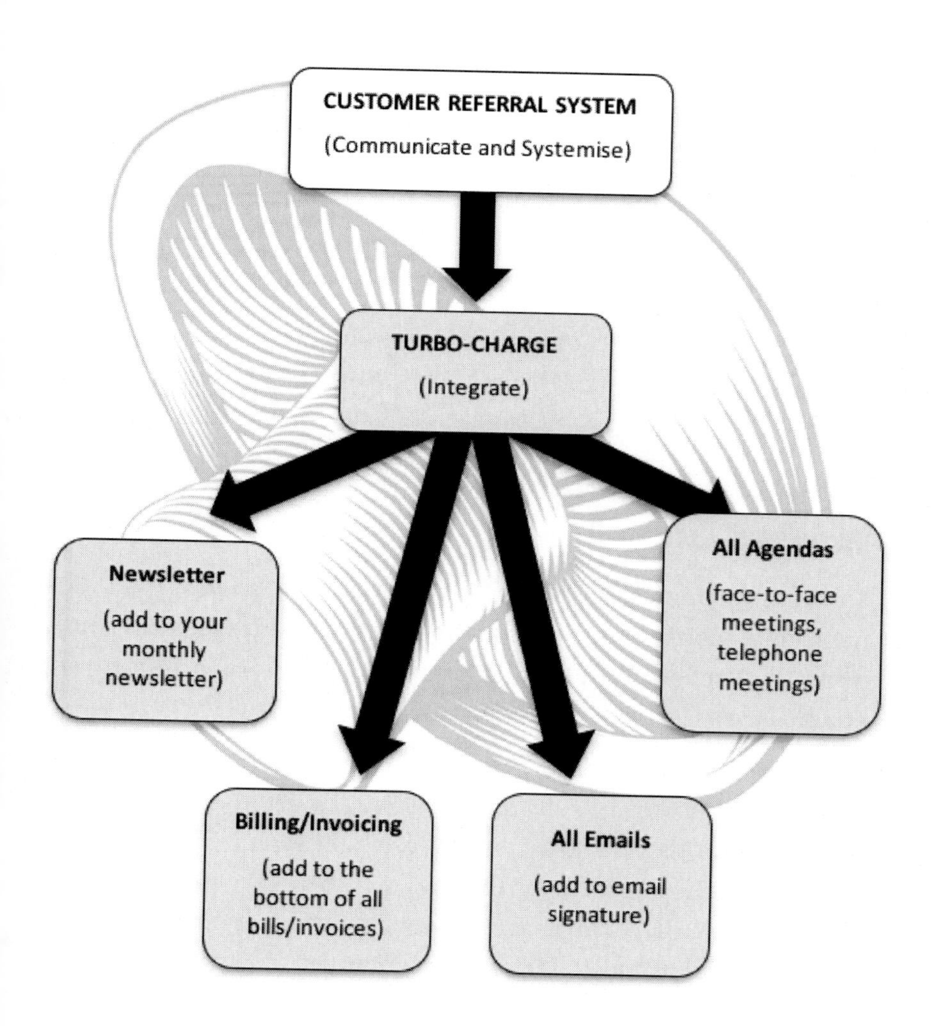

Again, you just need to add the referral incentive with a call to action. For example:

`'Free Fees for 12 Months by Referring Others to Us - Ask Us for More Details'`

Add to your monthly newsletter

Adding your referral message to the bottom of each page in your monthly printed newsletter is a great way to reinforce your referral programme.

In fact, your newsletter is an excellent place to add case studies from clients who have referred other people to you.

Okay, you're cooking on gas now. Let's now look at 'Increasing the Average Order Value' with *Up-Selling* and *Cross-Selling*...

Up-Sell and Cross-Sell

Up-selling and cross-selling are two of the easiest yet most neglected tactics that can instantly add hundreds, thousands, even hundreds of thousands of pounds of pure profit to any business.

Perhaps the best way to explain what an up-sell is is to give you a well-known up-sell that McDonald's use. Let's say you go into McDonalds and ask for any of their standard meals. The reply from the person serving you will be, 'Do you want to go large?' Basically, they are using a well-rehearsed 'Up-sell Statement' that makes it easy for the buyer to say 'yes'.

With just six carefully crafted words, McDonald's generate an up-sell that 30%–40% of customers say 'yes' to. That's another 30–40 people in every hundred that spend, say, a pound more than they would have done had the Up-sell Statement not been used.

And just think for a moment ...

The cost to McDonald's for providing the larger-sized meal probably adds up to about 10p – so they've just created another 90p of profit on the sale with virtually no effort (six words).

So to define up-sell more accurately:

An up-sell is when you move the customer up to a larger quantity (bigger size, etc.) of the same product or service for a perceived preferential price.

Let me now explain cross-selling. Let's use the McDonald's example again to demonstrate how the cross-sell works.

You go into McDonald's and ask for any of their main dishes, such as a Big Mac, or Chicken Sandwich. The reply from the person serving you will be, 'Would you like fries with that?' Basically, they are using a well-rehearsed *cross-sell statement* that makes it easy for the buyer to say 'yes'.

So to define cross-sell more accurately:

A cross-sell is when you sell a complementary product or service to the product or service initially being bought.

Ideally, be sure your cross-sell adds related value to your customer's purchase, and you can't go too far wrong.

So why do the up-sell and cross-sell work so well?

The reason why they work so well is that the up-sell or cross-sell statement is used only after the person has made the decision to buy. That means they are comfortable with their decision. It's at this point they are much more susceptible to the up-sell (or cross-sell), because they are in 'buying mode'.

You should be aiming to convert upwards of 30% of people with the up-sell or cross-sell.

Let me give you a simple example of how effective this can be. A client runs a fast-food outlet for a successful franchise called Le Petit Four Français. They were going along and building nicely, until Greggs (one of their biggest competitors) moved into the restaurant hall. Already there were the likes of McDonald's, KFC and many other fast-food outlets, but when Greggs moved in with their superior marketing muscle, sales plummeted.

So to reverse the trend, the primary thing we did was to introduce up-sells and cross-sells. Like so many businesses, Le Petit Four Français weren't offering any up-sells or cross-sells, so I told Michael, the owner of the franchise, to list his top seven best-selling food items, and then to link an up-sell or a cross-sell to each one.

I then told him to create a simple up-sell or cross-sell statement to each one and train the staff. Staff were then incentivised on the number of times a customer would up-sell or cross-sell. The results were staggering (but not surprising, not to me anyway).

Despite the added competition and a reduced footfall to the store, after three short months, sales were up three times based on the previous year (and that was before Greggs entered the fold).

That's the power of using up-sell and cross-sell.

Here are some more examples to get your juices flowing.

Example 1: Tri-creaser Deluxe Up-sell

The Tri-Creaser Deluxe up-sell actually changed my mindset on what an up-sell could achieve. Earlier I mentioned you should be looking for a minimum take-up of 30% from your up-sell. The Tri-Creaser up-sell achieves sales of over 70%.

A high take-up of the up-sell, although fantastic news, should also set your alarm bells ringing and bring up two questions you need to answer:

1. Is the 'standard' product price too low? In this example, we price-tested the standard price many times, and the price point we set was the 'perfect price'.
2. Is the 'Deluxe Version' priced too low? Again, in this example, we price-tested increases, and results showed the price was right.

Having answered the above two questions, you may well be able to achieve even more increases in profit! Take a look at the order form on the next page. This is one of the early ones we developed for the US market...

Tri-Creaser Priority Order Form

"The Revolutionary Creasing Device That Totally Eliminates Fibre Cracking, And Takes Just Minutes To Set Up – Even By Inexperienced Operators"

Please complete your details below and return this form (with your cheque – if relevant) in the envelope provided. Alternatively please call us at [redacted] or fax us at [redacted] to place your order.

☐ *Yes!* Please send me your Device. I want to take advantage of all these benefits...

1. **No more fibre cracking – perfect jobs every time**
2. **Very quick set up time with no need for training or demonstration**
3. **All settings are automatically built into the design saving set up time and operator error**
4. **Creases as fast as the folding machine can run – 25,000 sheets per hour or more**
5. **No outsourcing of straight creasing jobs ever again, saving time and money – the Tri-Creaser pays for itself on average between 1 and 3 jobs**

☐ I am replying on or before __________, so please also send me my FREE Bonus Gift (Tech-ni-Strippers / Inserts)

YOUR ORDER

Please send me (please tick): ☐ Tri-Creaser ($597) ☐ Tri-Creaser De-lux ($792)

Quantity: __________

TOTAL AMOUNT OF ORDER: $ ________ (i.e. 2 Tri-Creaser's is $1194)

Please give us details about your folding machine: MAKE: __________

MODEL: __________

DON'T FORGET ALL MY TRI-CREASER'S COME WITH OUR UNIQUE FIVE TIERED RISK FREE MONEY BACK GUARANTEE (please see attached letter)

Name: __________ Company Name: __________

Address: __________

Zip: __________ Phone: __________

Please tick your payment method:
☐ Credit / Debit Card (Full Payment)
☐ Credit / Debit Card (½ now, ½ 45 days from now)
☐ Personal/Company Cheque – Full Payment (please make cheques payable to "Tech-ni-Fold Ltd")

☐ MasterCard ☐ VISA ☐ JCB ☐ Switch ☐ Solo ☐ VISA Delta ☐ VISA Electron ☐ Am Ex

Name on Card __________ Valid From (if applicable) ______ Issue No. (Switch) ______

Credit / Debit Card Number: ☐☐☐☐☐☐☐☐☐☐☐☐☐☐☐☐ Expiry Date: ☐

Signature: ☐

Thank you for your order!

As soon as we process your credit card details or deposit your cheque we'll rush your order to you (it takes 5 working days or less).

Tech-ni-Fold Ltd

Example 2: Car Model Up-sell

Possibly one of the best exponents of the up-sell is the car dealer salesmen in conjunction with car manufacturers. The manufacturers produce a basic model and a number of upgrade versions depending on the buyer's needs and wants.

You know yourself that when choosing a car you may fully expect to walk out of the showroom with the basic model only to walk out with a model two or three levels above!

Example 3: DELL™ Computer Up-sell

Most computer manufacturers are great at this, but Dell™ stand out from the crowd. Their low prices, coupled with attractive up-sell offers, make it very difficult for the buyer not to move up to a better, faster model.

Once again, although the up-sell on each model has an increase of impressive benefits, the costs to Dell™ for these improvements are minimal and again add considerable profit to their sales.

Example 4: The Sunglass Hut Cross-sell

Buy any designer pair of sunglasses from the Sunglass Hut and, when you go to pay, the shop assistant will draw your attention to four 'plastic balls' on the front of the counter (with a price of £10 clearly shown). Each one contains a different coloured cleaning cloth for the sunglasses. Their cross-sell script goes something like this:

'Thank you, Mr Jones. Because you are ordering today, would you like to choose any one of the cleaning cloths in front of you, and I'll add just £9.99 to your order?'

Note the following:

- The assistant has been well trained and uses the name of the customer by looking at the card passed to them.
- This is a simple one-sentence cross-sell.
- The cross-sell in this example is probably adding close to £9.50 in pure profit to the sale!

Example 5: Kitchen Devil's Knife Set

One of the things you should do is to spend 30 minutes or so each day watching channels such as QVC and The Shopping Channel.

These programmes have some of the best marketing strategies on show as they run through one after another infomercial.

Be careful, though: make sure your wife or husband or partner doesn't start watching, as well, or they'll be dragged in like the rest of them!

For example, the well-known infomercial selling the Kitchen Devil's Knife Set selling for about £300 is very powerful.

They have the chef literally throwing food in the air and landing on the knife to be split perfectly in two. When you order, this is what the telesales girl say:

'Mrs Jones, because you're ordering today we have a special offer on the Kitchen Devil's Presentation

```
Mount. Made of beautiful solid wood, it will show off
your knife set on any work service in your kitchen.
Can I add just £19.99 to your order?'
```

It's hard to turn that down, having just spent £300 on the knife set! Most people want to parade their new knives, and what better way than to have the perfect showpiece for them!

Three short sentences for an increase in profit of about £16.00, with a product that unquestionably complements the original purchase.

Example 6: Tailors

A store selling men's tailored shirts can offer matching cuff links, ties and collar-stiffeners.

Example 7: Lawn Care

Offer a pruning service, grass removal, weed removal from borders, etc., or how about a discount on leaf and snow removal in the winter if they agree to a contract for the season's lawn care?

Example 8: Amazon.com

Amazon were pioneers of the online cross-sell. Whenever you choose a product to buy, they back this up with other recommendations.

For example, 'buyers of this book also bought these books'. They also show complimentary products or services alongside your chosen item ('Frequently Bought Together' and 'Customers Who Bought This Item Also Bought'), making it even easier for you to add-on other purchases. Here's a good example:

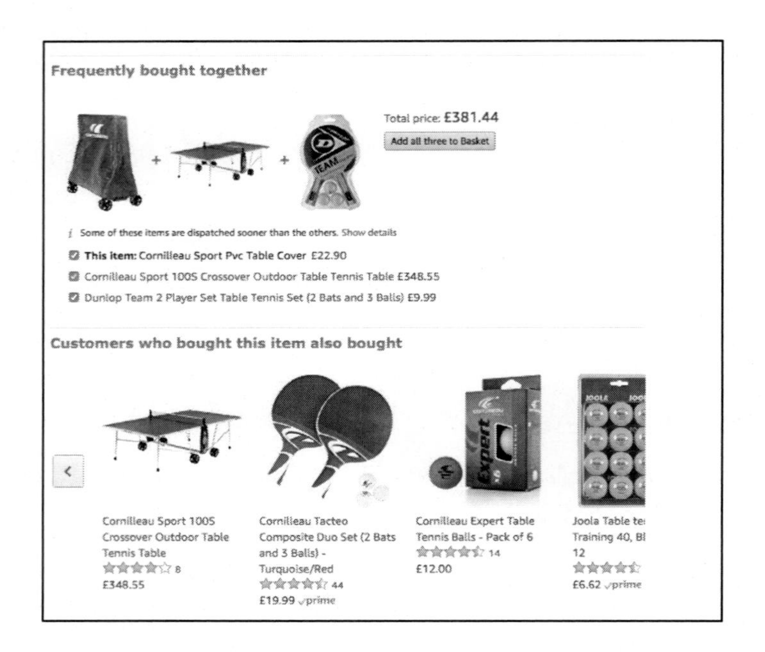

Example 9: Any Other Product or Service Sold by Your Business

The beauty of cross-sell is that it gives you the opportunity to sell other complementary products or services the business is selling. But there will be many more products and services you can include once you start thinking about it.

The important point to take from this is to look for the opportunities in the business to present related products or services. Then, offer these additions at a discount as a cross-sell.

In many cases, you'll find that some customers will want these products or services, but hadn't thought about buying them, either because they didn't think about needing that product or service at that time or didn't relate that need with their current need. Either way, you helped both them and you receive extra benefit.

Be aware of opportunities in the business to sell additional products or services to customers at the time of their initial purchase (and of course after this). Taking advantage of this opportunity will increase the sales and profits of the business within a very short space of time, with very little effort and no extra cost!

Let's now look at the last area for maximising customer value: *Reducing Attrition…*

Monthly Printed Newsletter

I've mentioned using a monthly printed newsletter several times already, and with good reason. It is one of the powerhouses of growing any business. It helps to retain your clients, customers or patients, of course, but it also helps to get customers buying more often and referring more often.

But, of course, there is a right and wrong way to do it.

Most people that produce a newsletter do it all wrong. The syndicated newsletters that are already done and re-branded are also done wrong.

There are three underlying principles that will ensure your newsletter becomes an amazing business growth tool for you.

Firstly, you must produce it monthly.

Secondly, you must physically print and mail a hard copy to your clients, customers or patients.

And finally, you must make it readable.

That's the key to success with your own printed newsletter.

I should know. I've been producing newsletters for 20 years now (see my first-ever issue on the next page). Right now, I personally write three newsletters each month.

I've advised hundreds of business owners on their own newsletters.

Over the years I've learned what works and what doesn't. Those three principles are the bedrock of a successful newsletter, and as long as you remember those three things, your success is guaranteed.

On top of these three vital principles, there are, of course, a number of important elements that contribute to making your newsletter successful. So, as an extra bonus for investing in this book, I've created a step-by-step guide for you titled, *The Anatomy of a Successful Newsletter*. You can download it for free here:

www.FreeFormulaBook.com/resources

***

POWER Marketing Succes

Practical, Proven, And Cost-Effective Growth Strategies For Your Service Busi

HUMOROUS BUSINESS QUOTE OF THE MONTH

cannot give you a formula for ccess, but I can give you the rmula for failure: Try to please erybody."

- Herbert Swope

MOTIVATIONAL BUSINESS QUOTE OF THE MONTH

he best executive is the one who s sense enough to pick good en to do what he wants done d self-restraint enough to keep m meddling with them while ey do it."

- Anon

Inside This Issue

e Front Page:
crease Your Response To Sales tters By More Than 500% With A mple Telephone Call...
age 1

e Critique Centre:
les Letters - For Once A Good ample...
age 3

ok Of The Month
llion Dollar Mailings -
nison Hatch
age 5

e Back Page:
WER Advertising: How To Choose e Best And Potentially Most ofitable Publications...
age 8

Increase Your Response T Sales Letters By More Than 500% With A Simpl Telephone Call

Hello You POWER Marketing Genius,

I was reminded today by a client that much of what I talk about (and write) is basic common sense. 'That's true' was my reply, 'but when it comes to sales and marketing, common sense isn't that common!'

Now I know that's a sweeping statement and because you're reading PMS I'm sure you certainly don't lack in the common sense department. But do you?

Are you one of the lousy 75 percenters, o are you one of the motivated 25 percenters

Answer me honestly...

Do you scrutinise every edition of PMS? Do you apply what I tell you?

Or do you do what regrettably 75% of people do - and simply do nothing? Are you a 25 percenter or one of the lousy 75 percenters?

This is the first step of common sense. If you don apply what you discover i every page of PMS then you're wasting your time. More importantly you're missing the opportunity t grow your business quick and easier than you could imagine!

All this stuff works. No. I rephrase that - it works bloody well.

Anyway, back to the common sense thread - enough of the lecture!

The reason I mentioned this in the first place is because this lead article talks about the merits of following up with a telephone call after sendi your sales letter or information pack.

That concludes this chapter. I've taken you through the various areas that will help you to maximise your customer value.

No matter what business you're in, you can capitalise on each of these four areas. I promise that you won't believe how easy it is to grow your business, as long as you apply these tactics and strategies to maximise the value of each client, customer or patient.

Now let's move on to the final part of THE FORMULA: 'Systemise' (you're going to love this)...

Chapter Summary

- Acres Of Diamonds: This part of the formula focuses on increasing the value of each client, customer or patient.

- 4 Key areas to do that:

    1. Increase the frequency of purchase
    2. Increase referrals
    3. Increase the average order value
    4. Reduce attrition (customer losses)

- 11 proven low-cost strategies to increase customer value:

    1. Moments of Truth
    2. Monthly Customer Prize Draw
    3. Customer Penetration System
    4. Customer Offer of the Month
    5. Up-Sell
    6. Cross- Sell

7. Reactivate Past Customers
8. Referral System
9. Customer Welcome Letter
10. Dealing with Complaints
11. Monthly Customer Newsletter

Creating Your 'Maximising Customer Value' System

Step 1: Transform existing tactics and strategies

Step 2: Use Moments of Truth to build an amazing customer experience

Step 3: Create and activate at least one maximising tactic and strategy for each of the four customer maximisation areas

For example...

- Customer Penetration System
- The Referral System
- Up-Sell and Cross-Sell
- Monthly Printed Newsletter

CHAPTER 8:

SYSTEMISE

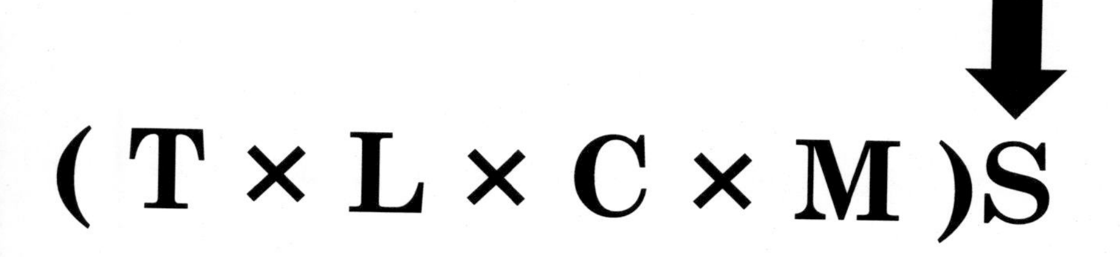

= EXPONENTIAL BUSINESS GROWTH

o far we've covered the first four components of THE FORMULA. They are the backbone of your entire business. As I mentioned earlier, they will provide you with...

Solidity

Growth

Profit

...and ensure your business is *immune to outside forces,* such as the competition and an ever-changing economy.

However, to take it to an even higher level, one that accelerates your growth even faster, you need to *systemise* and then *automate* these four components.

As I said earlier, often one of the real drawbacks of running a small or medium sized business (and you know this all too well) is that there just aren't enough people in the business to do everything that's required, so you end up working long hours, which impacts on every other area of your life.

By systemising and then automating the growth of your business, you reduce the reliance on people, free up a huge chunk of time for yourself and ensure your business keeps moving forward at pace.

Furthermore, systemisation and automation reduce mistakes <u>and</u> enhance results.

So it's a *win-win-win.*

But your burning question now will be:

How do I systemise and automate without needing to be a professor of sorts or needing expensive software?

Using today's technology and a bit of common-sense, this is possible, and you can do it quite easily.

I'm not saying you'll be able to automate absolutely everything, but much of your growth can be put on autopilot, and that's what this chapter focusses on.

Let's get started...

The 'Growth Continuum'

The first thing you need to recognise is that the three components of 'L' – Lead Generation, 'C' – Conversion and 'M' – Maximising Customer Value, should be part of a sequential system in your business.

You generate leads ...

You then convert those leads into sales ...

You then maximise the value of each customer ...

... and so the sequence continues.

Each of these three stages (as you've already discovered) can then be 'T' – Transformed.

If you've followed THE FORMULA so far, the great news is you already have a set of 'systems' in place. We just need to automate as much of them as possible. Agreed?

There are a number of ways to do this, of course. I'm going to explain how we do it and how we advise our clients to do it. The point is that you can systemise everything and automate a large chunk of the 'Growth Continuum', no matter what type of business you run. Some businesses can be completely automated, others need human intervention. In most cases, the latter will be the reality, but either way, your goal is two-fold:

Firstly, to systemise the three elements of 'L', 'C' and 'M' in THE FORMULA. We've done this already.

And secondly, to automate as much of each system as possible.

Surprisingly, neither is a challenge, you just need to commit to doing it.

If you DON'T DO IT, you'll still have an extremely successful business as long as you've implemented the first four sections of THE FORMULA. But systemising and automating them will help you build the business far quicker, and when/if you decide to exit the business at some point in the future, your business will be worth considerably more if you've automated as much of THE FORMULA as possible.

Here's how to automate as much of your systems as possible...

Automating Your Lead Generation

I spoke earlier about the critical importance of having an irresistible offer in all your lead-generation tactics and strategies. We spoke about how effective lead magnets are in getting people interested in your products or services.

So, let's first look at how you would make this process fully automated.

Your lead magnet is a special report. You create a landing page on your website (as detailed earlier) and people have to enter their first name and email address to gain access to it.

You then use an autoresponder (explained earlier) to automatically follow up with the prospect. Your free report and your follow-up sequence are focused on converting the prospect into a lead, whatever a lead is for you. It could be a meeting, a phone call, a free trial or a sale. Whatever it is, you make it irresistible to your Customer Avatar. With me so far?

You then create and launch the various lead-generation tactics and strategies (discussed earlier), whose sole objective is to get people to your landing page, enter their details and get the free report.

You then let your lead-generation tactics and strategies run, but whilst they're running, you're testing and improving them using the Core Elements.

What you've done, unwittingly, is to create a fully automated system. Yes, you have to implement the lead-generation strategies and then transform them, but 80% of your lead generation is now fully automated. All you've used is a landing page (remember, open 24/7) and an autoresponder (like AWeber) which also runs 24/7.

You'll now get leads even when you sleep or go on holiday ...

... and you've automated the lead-generation part of THE FORMULA.

Automating Your Conversion

Admittedly, automating the lead-generation part of your business is surprisingly easy. Once that part of the system churns out a lead, you now need to convert it. This can be slightly more complex.

If you're running an online business, then this process can and should happen seamlessly as you build your site to accept orders. You've probably already nailed this part of your business if that's the case.

But if your business needs to have a 'conversation' with your potential customers, clients or patients, then clearly, as you can't (yet) put in place robots to take the place of a human being, there needs to be human intervention to help convert that lead into a customer.

So, let's say you run a HR company and you place staff in care homes. Once the lead is generated, you or a member of your team would then go out to the prospective client in an effort to make the sale.

You could be a roofing specialist, a kitchen company, an electrician or whatever. The point is that you do need people involved in the process.

Now remember, if that is the case, you've already put in place your sales conversion system (back in Chapter 6), so you just need to automate the process as much as possible.

By that, I mean you automate the timing of each step in the system, and then, as you've already done, each step that can't be automated needs a step-by-step system that is followed.

To automate a sequence like this that involves more than just email automation, you need to use a piece of software that has what's known as 'automated processes' built in.

In my early businesses we used a piece of software called 'Goldmine' to do this, and it worked perfectly well, but for over 10 years now we've used Infusionsoft. As I said previously, it was a little complicated, but as it's gone through various versioning, it's now pretty easy to use, and it's a complete CRM system that will help you run your entire business.

You simply pay a monthly fee, depending on the number of users you have, and then you can start creating your automation (amongst many other things). It doesn't matter what software you use, the point is that as long as it includes automated processes, you can automate much of the conversion system.

All you do is transfer your paper-based sales conversion system (you should have completed your Sales Conversion System Design Table) and transfer it to your software of choice.

The hard yards were done creating your sales conversion system in the first place. You just transfer it into the software programme, and hey presto! You've now got an automated sales conversion system.

To explain this further, let's revert back to my completed Sales Conversion System Design Table in Chapter 6 (shown again on the next page). Notice I've now filled in the timeline for each element.

This is what the automation will look like inside your CRM system.

My Completed Sales Conversion System Design Table

DAY	CONTACT	OBJECTIVE
LEAD GENERATED		
0	Receive in-bound call (or make out-bound call)	
	Partner speaks with prospect	
STAGE 1: Meeting Arranged		
0	Email details of meeting	
1	Send confirmation letter	
3	Send Surprise Package	
STAGE 2: Reception Greeting		
0	Receptionist greets prospect	
	Offer refreshments	
	Partner greets prospect	
STAGE 3: The Meeting		
0	Follow meeting sales process	
	Ask for the order	
STAGE 4: Post Meeting		
0	Meeting follow-up letter	
3	Follow-up phone call	
5+	Follow-up system	
SALE & NEW CUSTOMER ACQUIRED		
MAXIMISING CUSTOMER VALUE SYSTEM		

LEAD GENERATED

- A call comes into the office. The people answering the phones have an optimised call answering script, which is pre-loaded into the CRM system for them to read (the reality is that you get the staff answering the phones to learn the script so it sounds natural, but it's still there for reference inside the CRM system). A new contact record is created, and the details required are input into the record for this lead.
- The lead is then passed on to an available partner who uses the qualification questionnaire (loaded as a form inside the CRM system) to determine the quality of the lead and to arrange a meeting.

STAGE 1: Meeting Arranged

- Once the meeting has been arranged and the call ended, the partner presses the complete button on the form, which automatically triggers the next sequence of events.
- The email confirming the meeting is merged with the relevant data entered into the form (such as the first name of the lead, the date and time of the meeting, and so on) and sent 15 minutes later.
- One day later, the confirmation letter is triggered by the CRM system and automatically merged, and the secretary prints it out on the company's letterhead, inserts it into a window envelope, affixes a stamp and then adds it to the mail pile for the post office later that day.

- Three days later, the Surprise Package covering letter is triggered by the system as above. The secretary adds the additional information to make up the package, inserts it into a large brown envelope and places it on the mail pile.

STAGE 2: Reception Greeting

- Each morning the CRM system shows which leads are coming to the office for a meeting and at what time. The reception area is primed and staged as per the instructions detailed in the CRM system. The partner reviews the contact's details stored in the CRM ready for the meeting.
- The receptionist greets each person (detailed in the CRM system) and offers them a drink from the drinks menu. They note their favoured drink on the form and later enter those details in the form ready for the next time the lead (or hopefully client) returns to the office.
- The partner is informed automatically by the system, once the drink details have been entered, that the lead is in reception.
- The partner waits a couple of minutes and then greets the lead.

STAGE 3: The Meeting

- The meeting room has already been 'staged' by the receptionist as per the instructions in the CRM system. That includes making sure the flip chart has paper, that the computer set up for television ready for presentation, that the speakers are working for video, etc.

- The partner then follows the 'Meeting Sales Process', as detailed in the CRM system. Obviously, the partner will have learned this system and won't be referring to the CRM system during the meeting.
- At the end of the meeting, the partner asks for the order.

STAGE 4: Post-Meeting

- Assuming the lead didn't convert into a client at the meeting, the partner enters the additional details gained during the meeting into the 'Meeting Form' in the CRM system, and once the 'enter' button is clicked, the CRM system takes over. It merges and prints the 'Meeting Follow-Up Letter', ready for the receptionist to mail.
- Three days later the CRM system alerts the partner to make the follow-up call. The partner uses the script in the CRM system.
- If the lead hasn't converted into a client at this stage, the CRM system then fulfils the follow-up sequence already entered into it.
- Once the lead becomes a client, the receptionist opens their contact record, changes them from lead to client, and then the 'Customer Maximisation System' takes over, again automated by the CRM system.

IMPROVE

- Remember, as I said previously, now your Sales Conversion is a system, each stage can be improved and optimised. Make sure you keep improving each stage using the Core Elements, so your conversion gets better and better.

As you can see, what we've done is automate the sales conversion system using your CRM software. Believe me, this is not difficult to set up. The hardest part is completing your Sales Conversion System Design Table (and even that's not difficult!). But once you've done that, it's just a case of transferring your hard copy into your CRM system, and then you're on your way.

Beautiful!

Automating Your Maximising Customer Value

You've now successfully automated the lead-generation and conversion parts of THE FORMULA. All that's left is to automate the final piece of the jigsaw (and arguably the most important).

As soon as you have a customer you need to automate the Moments of Truth steps you have already completed, and then automate the tactics and strategies you're using to maximise customer value.

Once again, you're going to use your CRM system to do this, just like you've done with your conversion system.

Firstly, you're going to transfer the hard copy details from your Moments of Truth Design Table to your CRM system.

You're then going to add the additional maximising customer value tactics and strategies to it, to ensure you maximise the earning potential from every client, customer or patient.

For example, if you've created various up-sell and cross-sell scripts, these will also be in the CRM system, and staff will have been trained on them, so that at the point of purchase the scripts are delivered to the customer to maximise the value and profit of the sale.

As mentioned above, once the lead converts into a client, customer or patient, their contact record in the CRM is changed from 'lead' to 'customer', which then triggers the sequence.

Automating Your Entire Business

This is beyond the scope of this book, but as you've already seen, we've already automated a huge chunk of your business. My advice is that you also look to systemise and automate the rest of your business, so it works like a well-oiled machine. The benefits are enormous, and you'll have a business that is more enjoyable for you, for your staff and for your clients, customers or patients.

More importantly, you'll create efficiencies all over the place. Profits will increase, and, as I said earlier, when you decide to exit you'll have a 'business-in-a-box' ready to sell for a top-end multiple!

Conclusion

Very few small or medium sized businesses have systemised and automated their growth like I've just shown you.

It doesn't matter what type of business you run. Whether it's online or offline, or bricks and mortar, this is a proven model that works time and time again. Once you automate, it frees you up to start doing the things you want to do in your business and in your life!

... and best of all ...

It enables you to further ACCELERATE the growth of your business by putting THE FORMULA on steroids!

All that's left now is to solve your single biggest problem...

Chapter Summary

- The first four components of THE FORMULA ensure that your business is immune to outside forces, such as the changes in the economy and competition.
- You need to systemise and then automate the 'L', 'C' and 'M' elements of THE FORMULA to further accelerate the growth of your business.
- Automation reduces your dependence on people, it frees up a huge amount of your time, it reduces mistakes and enhances results.

CHAPTER 9:

YOUR BIGGEST PROBLEM ... SOLVED

I hope you've enjoyed this journey so far with me. I appreciate you may be feeling overwhelmed at the moment (there's a lot to take in), but if you apply just a fraction of what I've revealed to you in this book, you'll have a more successful business ... guaranteed.

THE FORMULA works.

It can't be broken.

Just one of the tactics and strategies I've detailed can have a major effect on your growth.

However, in all my 20 years of helping business owners to grow their firms, there are three things, three big problems, that hold most of them back.

Firstly, they don't have the time to put in place THE FORMULA and the corresponding strategies for each of the five components.

You see, as the owner of a small or medium sized business, you often have to wear several hats. Whether you like it or not, you don't have the time to really dedicate yourself to marketing and growing your business. That means you'll rarely build the business to its full potential.

Secondly, they don't have the expertise to create and then implement the tactics and strategies.

Let's face it, you're an expert in what you sell. But you're unlikely to also be an expert in marketing and growth. That's not a criticism; that's just reality. You're rightly so immersed in your business that learning a whole new discipline just isn't feasible. Consequently, results from the marketing tactics and strategies you deploy seldom reach the heights they could.

And finally, business owners don't have surplus cash to spend on testing, refining and optimising all their sales and marketing.

If you're like most of the business owners I know, you are highly motivated to grow your business (because it brings you the rewards for setting it up in the first place), but you don't want to spend (and waste) thousands on testing what works and what doesn't. Right?

I realised some time ago that no one had successfully overcome these BIG problems for the owners of small and medium sized businesses.

Therefore, my team and I have worked day and night over the last few years, to create an "all-in-one" solution that's easy to apply, cost-effective and also guaranteed to be successful for any business owner who applies it.

It's called **'The Core Asset Vault'**.

It is a remarkable and totally unique online resource that includes more than 50 proven sales and marketing tactics and strategies that ANY small or medium sized business can use. I've covered only a fraction of them in this book.

You can forget about wondering how to implement THE FORMULA into your business, or how to create and implement the various powerful strategies. All are included in The Core Asset portal ready for you to quickly and easily apply to your own business.

Furthermore, to make it even easier for you to apply THE FORMULA and the relevant strategies into YOUR business, we've created 'Implementation Plans' which guide you through the whole process automatically, without you wondering what needs to be done first, second, third and so on.

We've got implementation plans to suit every business type, depending on whether you predominantly sell products, services, operate a retail store (online or offline) or run a restaurant.

... and here's the best part:

Each of the 50+ tactics and strategies has its own 'PLAYBOOK', complete with a step-by-step guide, overview video, fill-in-the-blank templates and working examples. When you use the PLAYBOOKS, it makes it an absolute cinch for you to create the relevant tactics and strategies for your business, and do it so they're successful right from the moment you launch them. More importantly, it reduces the time it takes to implement each strategy by around 95%!

If you can follow a simple cake recipe, you can follow each PLAYBOOK with ease.

Each one is constantly being updated to ensure it's the best it can be for you, and once we've proven a new strategy we create a PLAYBOOK for it and then add it to the relevant section of The Core Asset. In other words, you'll always have immediate and 24/7 access to what's working RIGHT NOW for small and medium sized businesses everywhere.

An Example of One of the Step-By-Step 'PLAYBOOKS'

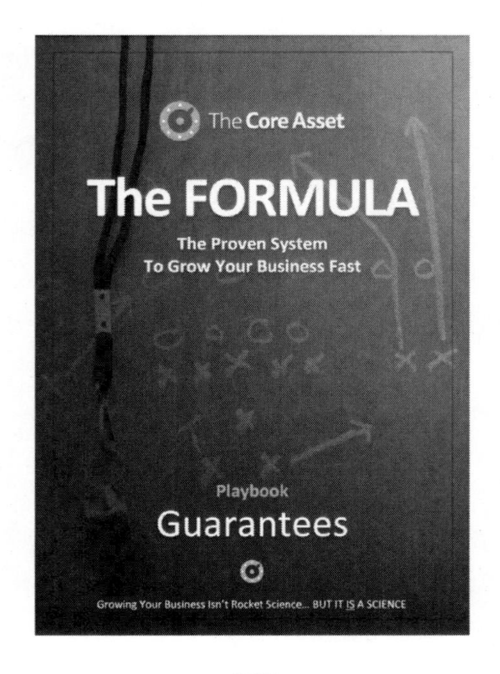

The Core Asset Vault therefore takes care of the three BIG challenges you face when growing your business: time, expertise and cash!

However, I've found that whilst The Core Asset Vault is an amazing resource and will undoubtedly help you grow your business quicker than you've ever done before, there's still a missing piece of the jigsaw, a piece that will guarantee your success: having an outside expert working by your side to drive you forward, act as a sounding board and, yes, make you accountable.

You need your own world-class Business Growth Mentor.

This is one of the success secrets. Many of the most successful entrepreneurs use a business coach or mentor to help them accelerate the growth of their business and improve their own performance. However, world-class coaching and mentoring has always been priced way too high for any small or medium sized business.

You see, as the owner of a small or medium sized business, you've been neglected by the large coaching and consulting organisations. Their fees are priced in the several thousand every month, which prices most small and medium sized businesses out of the market. These organisations prefer to work with large businesses with fat wallets and less accountability. Yet the small and medium sized business sector, no matter which country you're in, accounts for around 95% of the entire business market.

With that in mind, when Peter and I set up The Core Asset Vault, we did it with one single objective:

to bring world-class AND affordable business mentoring to small and medium sized businesses.

That's why we created the SALES ACCELERATOR Programme.

A programme unlike anything you may have ever seen or used before, for two primary reasons:

Firstly, it includes full 24/7 access to The Core Asset Vault itself and everything I've just explained.

And secondly, you get your very own world-class Business Growth Mentor as your personal Core Asset Vault guide, virtually guaranteeing your success.

The Sales Accelerator Programme has been built with you in mind: a busy business owner who wants to achieve better results, but doesn't have the time, expertise, inclination, energy and resources to continually test and measure new strategies to get there.

Furthermore, being an entrepreneur can be a lonely place, but with your very own, personal Business Growth Mentor by your side, you'll always have the support, motivation and expertise to ensure your success.

Better still...

As a thank you for investing in this book and taking the time to read through it, I have an even better offer for you! You can get the Sales Accelerator Programme for ***considerably less than the normal price*** (saving thousands).

Plus, it **includes over £10,000 worth** of valuable and unique business growth bonuses.

With that in mind, and to give you all the details, I've created a FREE value packed webinar titled, ***"How To Add An Additional 7-Figures To Your Business In The Next 12 Months Without Wasting Valuable Time, Spending A Fortune On Marketing, Or Having To Become A Marketing Pro"***.

You can register for FREE here:

www.TheFormulaWebinar.com

Want To Join Our Team Of Successful Business Growth Mentors?

Being a Business Growth Mentor is a very rewarding career, especially when you're part of a team and you have all the world-class tools and resources we've put in place. Find out how we can help you transition into a successful Business Growth Mentor here...

www.BusinessMentoringSystem.com

CHAPTER 10:

CONCLUSION ... ACCELERATE

Phew! You've just completed a full-on course on how to grow your business so you can get what you want out of it. Remember, new marketing tactics and strategies will emerge. Others will go. But THE FORMULA will never change. And now it's **YOUR FORMULA**.

Keep your building blocks in place, and work tirelessly to ensure you're capitalising on every part of THE FORMULA.

Look at what you're doing right now, and apply the Core Elements to transform your results. Add new lead-generation strategies and transform them. Add new conversion strategies and transform them. Add new maximising customer value strategies and transform them. Then systemise and automate them all to accelerate your growth even more.

You have the framework to do that. You just have to make the time and put the effort in, and you'll have a truly powerful business-building system that, in time, will transform your business.

This book is in itself a 'PLAYBOOK'. Don't read it just once. Read it over again and again. Make notes. Treat it like your own personal 'coach' to guide you through to becoming more successful than you ever thought possible.

I urge you to apply THE FORMULA to your business as soon as you can. Add one tactic or strategy at a time and keep testing. Above all else, don't ever risk too much of your own money. Test small and, when a tactic or strategy works, spend a little more, and so on (but remember, most of the tactics and strategies I've taken you through in this book are **FREE to implement**).

Continual improvement, is the name of the game, and as long as you have THE FORMULA firmly entrenched in your business, you can't go wrong.

ACCELERATE YOUR BUSINESS

Some of those who got their hands on this book before it went to print asked me if I could take a look at their attempt to implement THE FORMULA and if I could evaluate their efforts.

Whilst they had made good progress, it wasn't difficult to see areas that, with a little tweak here and there, they could make significant gains. And sure enough, once they'd been pointed out, we were able to see dramatic changes in results, pretty much overnight.

That's what I love about what you've learned in these pages. Building a business isn't rocket science, but it helps to have someone who understands how the rocket works to get the best out of it.

If you'd prefer a more hands-on approach, where you want even more personalised help and support, I've created something special for readers of this book... **and it's completely FREE**.

Let me explain...

Over the last 7 years we've been developing an amazing piece of software called the ***'Sales Accelerator ROADMAP'***.

To my knowledge, it is the only programme of its kind that can break down all the sales and marketing components of any business and then using the special algorithm (developed through analysing thousands of businesses in hundreds of different industries) it evaluates the strengths and weaknesses of your sales and marketing and then provides a step-by-step 'ROADMAP' on the steps you need to take to transform what you're doing right now and what gaps you need to fill.

The whole process only takes around 30 minutes and as I said, for readers of my book, it's completely FREE. You can arrange your ***Free ROADMAP Analysis*** here...

www.SalesAcceleratorRoadmap.com

Thanks again for investing in this book and for reading it right to the end. I wish you all the success in the future.

Steve Hackney